SMART MONEY MAKEOVER

A STEP-BY-STEP GUIDE TO MOVING YOUR MONEY FROM PAIN TO PLEASURE

SMART Money Makeover - A Step-by-Step Guide to Moving Your Money from Pain to Pleasure

Copyright © 2025 by Forrest Huguenin

All rights reserved.

No part of this publication may be reproduced, stored in a retrieval system, or transmitted in any form or by any means—electronic, mechanical, photocopy, recording, or otherwise—without the prior written permission of the author, except in the case of brief quotations used in critical articles or reviews.

Published by Intentional Money Solutions Press

An imprint of Intentional Money Solutions, LLC

www.intentionalmoneysolutions.com

Cover design by Forrest Huguenin

Illustrations by Forrest Huguenin, powered by ChatGPT

Interior design by Forrest Huguenin

ISBN: 978-0-9777439-1-9

First Edition

Printed in the United States of America

This book is a work of nonfiction based on the author's personal experience, professional practice, and interpretation of financial strategies. While every effort has been made to ensure accuracy, the author and publisher make no guarantees regarding the results of applying the information contained herein. Financial situations vary. Readers are encouraged to seek professional advice specific to their circumstances.

For permissions, speaking engagements, or coaching inquiries, please contact:

info@intentionalmoneysolutions.com

I dedicate this book first of all to my son, whom I am very proud of. Michael, every father's wish is that his son go further and faster than he has. Based on where you are now, I have no doubt that you will do just that.

Next, I dedicate this book to a very special woman who literally walked into my life at a time when I least expected she would. You have motivated me and moved me to become a better man. You tell me that I can do amazing things and because of your incredible smarts and continuous encouragement, I do. And this book is one of those things. This book would not have appeared as it has, when it has, if it were not for you. You truly are a unicorn. And you are my muse. Thank you.

Also, to my parents. To my dad who worked HARD every day of his life. We never had a lot, but we always had what we needed, and sometimes a little more. He taught me to never walk away from your responsibilities, because a real man sticks it out. And to my mom who was always there for me, even when I messed up. She scrubbed floors and toilets so that four pain-in-the-butt boys could have what they needed, even when we didn't appreciate her the way we should.

To my many mentors, examples and guides who thought enough of me to share their precious knowledge because they believed I could be and do and have more. You have my deepest gratitude.

Finally, I dedicate this book to all those who struggled with money for so many years, who have tried "everything" but still haven't tamed the beast. I know how you feel and this book is for you, to give you hope and a plan. Because if I can overcome everything that life has thrown at me, including my own dumb money moves, you surely can. I believe in each and every one of you!

Table of Contents

Introduction: From Pain to Pleasure 1

Chapter 1: The Cost of Financial Shame 7

    CHAPTER 1 BONUS STORY: From Pain to Pleasure 11

Chapter 2: Self-Knowledge & Your Money Personality 15

    CHAPTER 2 BONUS STORY: The Mirror 27

Chapter 3: Monetary Awareness 31

    CHAPTER 3 BONUS STORY: The Numbers Don't Lie 37

Chapter 4: Allocated Spending 43

    CHAPTER 4 BONUS STORY: The Plan (or Lack of One) 51

Chapter 5: Ready Cash 55

    CHAPTER 5 BONUS STORY: When It Rains 61

Chapter 6: Targeted Credit Use & Your Debt Snowball 65

    CHAPTER 6 BONUS STORY: Credit Games 75

Chapter 7: The 30-Day SMART Money Makeover Challenge 79

    CHAPTER 7 BONUS STORY: All In 83

Chapter 8: High Walls, Wide Moat 87

    CHAPTER 8 BONUS STORY: The Shift 97

Chapter 9: Investing Without the Hype 101

    CHAPTER 9 BONUS STORY: Transitions 109

Chapter 10: Becoming the New You 113

    CHAPTER 10 BONUS STORY: Pleasure At Last 119

Bonus Section 123

- The Money Personality Assessment 123
- Money Conversation Starters 124
- Recommended Tools & Resources 126
- Dealing With Debt Collectors & Negotiating With Creditors ... 127
- Credit Score Boosting Tips 129
- Book Club / Small Group Guide 130
- Coaching & Next Steps 131

Final Words From Forrest 133
About The Author 135

Introduction: From Pain to Pleasure

I still remember the pants.

They were too tight. Too short. They belonged to a boy whose family my mother worked for. I was just a kid — maybe seven or eight — and I was already learning what it meant to feel *less than*. My dad was trying to wrestle me into those pants, probably doing the best he could with what we had. But I didn't care about his intention. All I knew was that they didn't fit — not just physically, but emotionally. They told me I was secondhand. Not enough. That other people had options, and I had whatever was left.

That moment stuck with me for years. It was about way more than pants.

It was about shame.

It was about lack.

And eventually, it was about rebellion — the kind that makes you spend more than you have just to prove to yourself (and the world) that you've made it.

This Isn't Just Another Money Book

I didn't write *SMART Money Makeover* to help you clip coupons, deprive yourself into submission, or hustle your way into burnout. I wrote this book because I've *lived* both sides of the financial spectrum — the pain of not having enough and the pleasure of creating more than I ever thought possible.

Introduction: From Pain to Pleasure

But the most powerful transformations I've seen — in my own life and in the lives of my clients — don't come from just budgeting better or earning more.

They come from finally understanding *why* you relate to money the way you do.
They come from shifting your identity, not just your spending.
They come from rewriting the invisible story you've been living out every time you swipe a card or avoid checking your bank account.

That's what this book is about.

Who this book is for

This book is for every person who knows they can do more, be more and have more.
It's also for everyone who is finally sick and tired of being sick and tired.
Lastly, it's for anyone who is tired of blaming everything and everyone around them for their situation and is ready to start taking charge of their own lives and their own money.

Who this book is NOT for

This book is not for someone looking for a quick fix.
It's also not for anyone looking to get rich without putting real work in, especially on themselves.
Finally, this book is NOT for anyone who can't put their big pants on and take personal responsibility for their own mess.

What "Pain to Pleasure" Really Means

Introduction: From Pain to Pleasure

Pain is overdraft fees, late-night anxiety, arguments about money, and that sinking feeling when payday hits but it still isn't enough. I know each of those pains and then some.

Pleasure is peace.
It's options.
It's knowing you can handle what life throws at you, not because you're lucky, but because you've built a system that works. It took me a lot of trial and error to figure that out.
It's buying what you want without guilt — not because you're being reckless, but because you planned for it. That part took some real internal rewiring.
It's being generous — not because you feel obligated, but because you *can*.

Financial pleasure is possible, and it starts with a makeover — not just of your money, but of your mindset.

What You'll Learn in This Book

In the chapters ahead, I'm going to walk you through a system I developed after years of coaching people just like you — entrepreneurs, business owners, side-hustlers, professionals and everyday people who are great at making money but secretly struggle to manage it.

It's called the **SMART Money System**, and it's built on five unchanging core principles:

- **S – Self-Knowledge**: Understanding your relationship with money and your money personality.
- **M – Monetary Awareness**: Knowing your numbers — income, expenses, net worth, and cash flow.

Introduction: From Pain to Pleasure

- **A – Allocated Spending**: Creating an intentional spending plan that reflects your values.
- **R – Ready Cash**: Building the right savings for emergencies, seasons, and long-term goals.
- **T – Targeted Credit Use**: Using credit strategically — never impulsively. And blasting away at debt that was accumulated unwisely.

These aren't just financial tactics. They're mindset shifts. Behavior resets. And ultimately, they're the blueprint for taking control of your money — and your life.

Please do the exercises where indicated. They are not just busy work. They are a critical part of remaking your mindset and your life.

Also, please follow the chapters in order and read the accompanying short-story.

Speaking of… I've also included something different, an extra treat for you: A very true-to-life short story chronicling the journeys of two people who may or may not seem familiar to you. You will come to know them both, Robert and Kia, in short installments showing each stage of their transformation at the end of each chapter. You can choose to read it, or not. You will still be able to follow the principles in this book regardless.

But, I guarantee you that should you choose to read their stories, they will touch a place in you that will make your own financial journey hit a bit differently. You will find that you identify in some way with either, or both, of these brave souls who are struggling to overcome their own shortcomings. Shortcomings that are common to so many of us. And it may just give you that little extra push and hope you need to take the actions you must take in order to finally transform your money experience from one of pain to that of pleasure.

Introduction: From Pain to Pleasure

One Last Thing Before We Start

I know what's it's like to be standing on the ledge, the abyss just below your feet, while it feels like forces beyond your control are pushing you from behind.

One vivid memory comes to my mind at this moment. ***It was 1991 and I was at the lowest point of my life.*** I'd lost my job. My car had just been repossessed. My in-laws at the time wanted to kick me out of the house we had been renting from them. And, I didn't have a clue about where my next dollar was going to come from.

And if that wasn't enough... my son had just been born! I remember holding him in my arms and saying *"Welcome to the world son. Daddy doesn't have a job."* And I started crying.

But, somehow in those darkest of moments, I found light. I also found the will to keep going. Yes, I fell, time and time again. I bruised myself over and over, I skinned my knees repeatedly and I took some blows that knocked the wind out of my soul.

There were times where I felt like I didn't have anything more left in me and I lost the will to go on. But, through all of that, somehow, I got back up. And I kept getting back up until I stood firm and unshaken, bruised but not broken, bent but unbowed. And I'm still standing.

I know in my heart of hearts that if I can make this journey, you can as well. This is your call to get up. Shake it off. Forget what they said about you. Forget your mistakes. Forget your past. You are here today and you are making a commitment at this moment to turn a new page and write the great comeback story of your life.

And, always remember these words:

Introduction: From Pain to Pleasure

You are not broken.
You are not behind.
You are not bad with money.
And you are not the sum of your bank accounts.

You've just never had a system that was designed to support the *real you*.
This book is that system.
I pray the knowledge inside its pages work for you as well as it has worked for me and the many others who have applied it in their lives.

Let's get started, my friend!

Chapter 1: The Cost of Financial Shame

I still remember those pants.

They were too small, too tight, too loud with the message they carried: *You don't belong. You don't have enough. You are less than.*

They didn't come from a store. They came from a family my mom worked for. Hand-me-downs that weren't handed down with dignity. Just passed along like leftovers — someone else's "used to be."

I didn't have the words for it then, but I felt it deep: embarrassment, lack, and a shame I couldn't name. That moment branded something into me. It told me that money wasn't just about numbers — it was about worth. About identity. About whether I had the right to feel proud in my own skin.

And if you're honest with yourself, you've got a version of that story too.

When the Story Starts with Shame

No one gets out of childhood without forming a relationship with money — even if the relationship is silence, stress, or survival mode. We don't talk about it much, but the truth is, most of our adult financial decisions are driven by emotional pain we haven't named yet.

We grow up and think we're making logical choices. But in reality? We're trying to out-run, out-earn, or out-spend a belief we picked up as kids: *I'm not enough. I don't have enough. I'll never be enough.*

Some of us try to prove ourselves with purchases. Some try to hide our insecurity with luxury. Some stay stuck in fear and scarcity, afraid to let money go, afraid we'll never get it back.

The result? We operate from a place of pain — not power.

Chapter 1: The Cost of Financial Shame

The Quiet Cost of Trying to "Look Rich"

Let me be real: I've made money, and I've messed it up.

There were years when I was earning well and still secretly broke. I had the car, the clothes, the lifestyle — but underneath all that was a guy trying to prove that the boy in the hand-me-down pants had made it.

It took me a long time to realize I wasn't spending for joy — I was spending for *justice*. To show the world that I had arrived. To rewrite the story of lack with shiny stuff.

But no amount of spending could fix what was broken on the inside. The high would fade, but the shame stayed. Until I faced it.

The Real Root of Money Problems

Listen, budgeting apps and spreadsheets are helpful — but they don't heal. They can't touch the invisible stories shaping your money habits. That's why I always say: **before we can make over your money, we have to understand your money story.**

Most people jump straight to strategy — "How do I get out of debt? How do I save more?" — without ever asking, "*Why* do I spend the way I do? What am I really trying to feel, or avoid?"

If you skip this step, any system you build will eventually fall apart. Because it's not your budget that's broken. It's the belief driving it.

Chapter 1: The Cost of Financial Shame

From Pain to Permission

This chapter is an invitation. To slow down. To look inward. To be radically honest with yourself — not from a place of guilt, but from compassion.

You're not "bad with money." You've just been carrying stories that were never yours to begin with. It's time to lay them down.

It's time to shift the focus from shame to self-knowledge.

In the next chapter, we'll dig into your **Money Personality** — the unique wiring that shapes your financial behaviors. But before we go there, I want to give you a simple exercise to help you begin shedding the shame and stepping into clarity.

Practical Steps Toward Healing

This isn't homework. This is healing work.

1. Reflect on Your Past
What early experiences shaped your view of money? Was it struggle? Abundance? Silence? Chaos? Write down two or three childhood memories that still stick with you today.

2. Identify the Pattern
What behaviors do you notice in your current money life? Overspending? Avoidance? Fear? Where might those connect to those early experiences?

3. Name the Story
Try to articulate the core belief underneath your financial habits. Maybe it sounds like, "I have to spend to feel seen," or "If I save money, something bad will happen." No judgment — just notice it.

Chapter 1: The Cost of Financial Shame

4. Challenge the Belief
Ask yourself: *Is this story true? Is it serving me?* What new belief would feel more empowering and true to who you're becoming?

5. Share It (If You're Brave)
Sometimes the best way to break shame is to speak it aloud. Share one insight from this exercise with someone you trust. Watch how powerful that small act can be.

This is where the makeover begins — not with money, but with meaning.

Let's keep going.

Next up: **Your Money Personality** — and why knowing it will change everything.

But, before we go there, please take a moment to read the first installment of our fictional story. We pick up with them both at their low points, deep in despair. Maybe you will see yourself in them. In any event, I'm pretty sure you will enjoy watching our characters take their journey from leaving pain behind and advancing toward pleasure…

Chapter 1: The Cost of Financial Shame

CHAPTER 1 BONUS STORY: From Pain to Pleasure

ROBERT

Robert sat on the edge of his mattress, scrolling through his bank app with a sinking feeling in his gut.

$92.16. That's all he had left — and rent was due in four days.

His phone buzzed.
A group text from his boys:

"Vegas next month. Let's run it back. YOLO."

Chapter 1: The Cost of Financial Shame

He sighed. That used to be him — bottle service, new Jordans, never missing a trip.
Now? He could barely afford gas.

He threw the phone on the bed and opened the mail.
Credit card past due. Utilities threatening to shut off.
And the worst part? He made decent money. But somehow, it never stuck.

He blamed the divorce. He blamed the economy.
He even blamed his ex for the car note he co-signed on.

"I just need to hustle harder," he muttered.

Maybe one of those finance YouTubers had the secret.
Or maybe he could flip sneakers again.
Or maybe, just maybe, one more loan would buy him time to figure it all out.

He lit a cigarette, looked around the cluttered room, and made a silent promise:

"I'm gonna fix this. On my own."

Chapter 1: The Cost of Financial Shame

KIA

Kia stared at her reflection in the bathroom mirror.
Eyes puffy. Hair wrapped. Shirt from a clearance rack she couldn't afford when she bought it. Divorce papers on the kitchen counter, still unsigned.

She was tired — not just physically, but soul-tired.
The kind that comes from pretending you're okay when you're anything but.

Rent was late. Again.
The daycare lady gave her a "gentle reminder" that she couldn't keep watching her daughter if she didn't catch up.

Chapter 1: The Cost of Financial Shame

She opened her laptop to apply for another "urgent cash" loan and paused.

There, in the corner of her browser, was a tab she forgot she'd left open:

"SMART Money Makeover – A Step-by-Step Guide to Moving Your Money From Pain to Pleasure."

She clicked.
Scrolled.
Read the description again.

"From pain to pleasure."
"Your story isn't over."
"You don't need perfect credit. You just need a decision."

She sat still for a moment.
Then opened her notebook and wrote:

This ends here.

Not just the bills.
The shame.
The silence.
The sinking feeling that she'd never get ahead.

Kia didn't know how long it would take.
She didn't know where she'd find the money.

But she knew one thing:

She was done surviving. It was time to rebuild.

Chapter 2: Self-Knowledge & Your Money Personality

Money doesn't just buy things.
It reveals things.
And more often than not, it reveals *you*.

Your choices — how you earn, spend, save, give, invest — all point back to one powerful force: **your money personality.**

This chapter is about self-awareness, not self-judgment. Because until you know why you do what you do with money, you'll stay stuck in cycles that feel frustrating and mysterious. But once you *see yourself clearly*, the path forward gets a whole lot easier.

You Are How You Spend

We like to think we're logical when it comes to money. But the truth? Most of us are emotional — deeply emotional.
And that's okay. That's human.

Your environment, family, culture, and experiences all shape how you relate to money. The stories you absorbed growing up — about success, sacrifice, pleasure, fear, risk, security — still echo in your adult choices.

This is why two people can have the same income, same expenses, same financial goals… and yet behave in completely different ways.

Because money isn't just about math.
It's about mindset, emotion, identity — and personality.

Chapter 2: Self-Knowledge & Your Money Personality

The 4 Money Personalities

After years of coaching people through financial transformation, I've discovered four dominant money personality types. These types aren't boxes — they're mirrors. You might see yourself clearly in one, or notice traits in a few. That's normal.

But usually, one of these types stands out as your default setting — your primary lens for making financial decisions.

Let's meet the types:

1. The Surfer – *The Free-Spirited Spender*

- **Core Belief**: "Life is short — enjoy it while you can."
- **Strengths**: Fun-loving, generous, lives in the moment
- **Challenges**: Impulse spending, retail therapy, hard time delaying gratification
- **Watch Out For**: Overspending to feel better, confusing "stuff" with satisfaction
- **Pro Tip**: Use tools like the 24-hour rule and cash-only systems. Build structure around your spontaneity without killing your joy.

---

2. The Soldier – *The Disciplined Defender*

- **Core Belief**: "Protect yourself. Plan ahead. Be smart."
- **Strengths**: Responsible, structured, risk-averse
- **Challenges**: Overly frugal, resistant to change, can over-insure or under-enjoy

Chapter 2: Self-Knowledge & Your Money Personality

- **Watch Out For**: Letting fear of "what if" rob you of "what is"
- **Pro Tip**: Budget for fun. Balance caution with opportunity. Give yourself permission to live a little.

3. The First Responder – *The Compassionate Giver*

- **Core Belief**: "If I have it, I should help."
- **Strengths**: Empathetic, generous, deeply caring
- **Challenges**: Self-sacrifice, financial enabling, guilt-based giving
- **Watch Out For**: Giving to others at your own expense, co-signing on poor decisions
- **Pro Tip**: You don't have to stop giving — just do it wisely. Set healthy boundaries and prioritize self-care.

4. The Hunter/Gatherer – *The Ambitious Entrepreneur*

- **Core Belief**: "Money is a tool to build my dreams."
- **Strengths**: Visionary, driven, risk-taker
- **Challenges**: Overcommitting, blind spots, neglecting relationships
- **Watch Out For**: Taking uninformed risks, hyper-focus on goals, burnout
- **Pro Tip**: Dream big, but don't leap without looking. Slow down to plan, assess, and protect what matters most.

Chapter 2: Self-Knowledge & Your Money Personality

No Type Is "Better" — Just Better Understood

There's no perfect personality. Every type has gifts. Every type has gaps. What matters is that you start working *with* your wiring, not against it. Once you know your type, you can:

- Choose strategies that actually suit your strengths
- Catch yourself before your blind spots bite you
- Communicate better with your partner or spouse
- Set goals that are actually achievable for *you*

Ready to Meet Your Type?

Now it's your turn.

Take the **IMS Money Personality Assessment** in the bonus section of this book. It's simple, intuitive, and designed to help you identify your dominant personality — fast.

☞ Once you finish, take a moment to reflect:

- What part of your type description hit home?
- How has this personality helped or hurt your finances?
- What's one belief you now recognize that needs to shift?

This is the *Self-Knowledge* piece of SMART — and it's the beginning of everything. You cannot move from pain to pleasure without knowing what's *really* driving your decisions.

Chapter 2: Self-Knowledge & Your Money Personality

Let's Get Real About Mindset

I stress the importance of mindset so much in my coaching and in this book because experience has told me that mindset is everything. And believe me when I tell you, I found that out the hard way.

I kept thinking that the answer to my problem was making more money. But every time I raised my income, those pesky money problems kept following me. What the heck?

It wasn't until I realized this that things began to turn around: I didn't have an income problem. I had a ME problem!

Aha! So, the bad news is that I was the problem, not the money.

Aha, again! The good news is that if the problem is me, I can also fix me, so the situation could get better. And thus began my journey away from pain and towards healing.

The 3 Different Money Mindsets

I have long known that rich people think differently about money than poor people. But, I didn't know that there was a middle-class way of thinking about money too. Thanks to a talk I heard Myron Golden give, I now have clarity on this topic. So, let me break it down as simply as I can.

Poor people believe the primary purpose of money is to make just enough to pay their bills and survive.

Middle-class people believe the primary purpose of money is to make enough to pay their bills on time so they maintain good credit in order to buy more of the things that they really can't afford in the first place, but, they can afford the payments.

Chapter 2: Self-Knowledge & Your Money Personality

Rich people, on the other hand, believe the primary purpose of money is to accumulate assets that generate income from which they can buy more assets which in turn generate more income. And from these proceeds, they live their lives on a high level.

Where are you in that spectrum? I was in the first two for most of my life.

It wasn't until I understood the rich person's view of money that I had my great awakening. It was at that point that I began seeking ways to put my money to work so that it can have babies that will grow up to have their own babies and continue the cycle.

It is crucial that at this point in your journey, you make the conscious decision to use money in such a way that it turns into more money. You have to get *intentional* about your spending.

Designer clothing and handbags are not going to turn into more money.

That Uber eats order is not going to turn into an income-producing asset.

Neither is that YOLO vacation your buddies want you to go on this weekend.

I once heard a very wise woman in the financial arena say, "If it's on your ass, it's not an asset!"

Now, the purpose of the previous few lines is not to disparage spending on the things you love. I am not a Scrooge.

On the contrary, I want you to spend on the things you love, to live a rich life.

But, I want you to do it intentionally. Have a plan that allows you to enjoy life today while building for a richer, brighter tomorrow.

Chapter 2: Self-Knowledge & Your Money Personality

You have got to stop spending your money buying things that depreciate in value. Instead, start looking for places to put your money that appreciate in value. Examples of this would be the stock market, real estate or a business.

I had achieved all 3 of these until I got divorced recently and lost the real estate in the divorce. Many of you know the pain of which I speak. Wink-wink. But, I am happy to say that I am hard at work to ensure I re-establish this crucial piece of my wealth plan.

Your Money Thermostat

Here is the other piece that was part of my great awakening when it came to money. It doesn't matter how much money you want or how much money you get. If the sum of money that comes into your hand exceeds your money thermostat, you will find a way to automatically bring your money back down to the preset level that makes you comfortable.

Let me illustrate. We all have thermostats in our homes. The purpose of the thermostat is to maintain a pre-determined temperature in your environment that makes you feel comfortable. You only have to set it once, and it will automatically regulate the HVAC system in your hoe to insure that temperature is maintained.

If the temperature gets too high, the thermostat will kick in and pour cold air into the room until the temperature comes back down to where you set it. If the temperature gets too low, such as in the winter, the thermostat will kick in and command the furnace to pour heat into the room until it gets back up to where you set it.

The question I have for you at this point is, where have you set your thermostat?

Chapter 2: Self-Knowledge & Your Money Personality

Is it set at $40k, $60k or $100k per year? It doesn't matter where you set it, because no matter where you set it whenever more money comes into your life than you feel comfortable having, your mental thermostat will kick in ands find a way to get rid of the excess until it comes back down to a level you are mentally comfortable with.

I was that person. Whenever larger sums of money would start flowing to me, I would always get nervous and wonder, "What bad thing is about to happen to take this money away from me?" And then I would promptly cause the bad thing to happen in one form or another so that the excess money went away and I was once again "comfortably broke."

This is why you constantly hear stories of lottery winners who win millions and millions of dollars, only to end up broke again a few years later.

So, my advice to you is to first become a millionaire in your mind, which will then translate to your habits. Then, when those millions come you will be able not only to keep them, but to grow them into many more millions!

Don't allow yourself to be "comfortably broke" like I was. Pick up a stick and beat broke away from your door with a vengeance!

🖋️ 💧 Raising Your Money Thermostat: 5 Shifts That Change Everything

Before the budget.
Before the debt plan.
Before the investing...

You've got to upgrade what's happening between your ears. Because **money doesn't grow faster than your mindset.**

Chapter 2: Self-Knowledge & Your Money Personality

Here are five mindset shifts to help you move from *scarcity* to *abundance* — and from stuck to building wealth with purpose:

---

1. Stop Saying "I Can't Afford That." Start Asking "How Can I Afford That?"

Scarcity shuts the door. Creativity opens it.
Start seeing money as a problem to solve — not a wall to fear.

---

2. Choose Ownership Over Victimhood

You may not be responsible for where you started — but you *are* responsible for what you do next. Wealth begins where blame ends.

---

3. Replace Instant Gratification with Long-Term Vision

Ask yourself: "Will this still matter in 5 years?"
Wealthy people play the long game — not just with money, but with their habits.

---

4. Upgrade Your Circle

Surround yourself with people who talk about growth, investing, ownership, and purpose — not just spending and complaining.
Environment feeds mindset.

Chapter 2: Self-Knowledge & Your Money Personality

5. Believe That Wealth Is *For You*

Not just for "them." Not just for rich families or influencers.
You are not an outsider to wealth. You're a **future owner**. A **builder**. A **legacy-maker.**

💭 "If your mindset doesn't match your vision, your money will never follow."

✏️ Mindset Reset: Journal Exercise

Now that you've seen how your personality and past experiences shape your behavior, it's time to intentionally reshape your thinking.

Take 10–15 minutes to complete this exercise. Be honest. Be bold. Be *you.*

---

1. What's the biggest money belief I inherited — and is it still serving me?

(e.g., "Money doesn't grow on trees." "People like me never get ahead." "Money causes problems.")

---

2. When I picture my wealthy future self, how do they think about money differently than I do right now?

---

3. What's one way I can shift my mindset this week?

(e.g., Repeat an affirmation daily, pause before spending, talk about money openly with someone I trust)

Chapter 2: Self-Knowledge & Your Money Personality

4. What would I do differently if I truly believed I was capable of building wealth?

💭 **Coach's Note:**
Your mindset is the thermostat for your financial life. If you don't reset it, everything will eventually slide back to "normal." But if you rewire your beliefs, your behaviors will follow — and that's where real transformation begins.

Coming Up Next:
In the next chapter, we'll go deeper into **Monetary Awareness** — learning how to clearly and confidently understand your numbers, without shame or confusion.

Let's build from the inside out.

Chapter 2: Self-Knowledge & Your Money Personality

Chapter 2: Self-Knowledge & Your Money Personality

CHAPTER 2 BONUS STORY: The Mirror

ROBERT

Robert always thought of himself as "good with money."

He paid bills (usually). He made decent money (on paper). He didn't buy dumb stuff (unless you counted the sneaker wall, the streaming subscriptions he never used, or the $300 cologne he hadn't touched in months).

But something wasn't adding up. Literally.

Chapter 2: Self-Knowledge & Your Money Personality

That night, he clicked a link from a podcast called *Real Money, Real Talk*. The guy said something that hit different:

"You don't have a money problem. You have a *relationship with money* problem."

He scoffed. "Relationship? I don't *love* money — I need it."

Still, he clicked through to a free quiz: *What's Your Money Personality?*

He answered the questions half-distracted... but the result?
The Surfer.

Impulsive. Avoids structure. Lives for the moment.
Struggles with planning. Often feels like money just disappears.

He stared at the screen.

"Damn."

He remembered his mom doing payday loans to buy school clothes. His dad blowing every tax refund on TVs or rims. Nobody ever taught him how to build — only how to float.

"But I'm not my parents," he whispered.

Still, the pattern was hauntingly familiar.
Maybe it wasn't just bad luck or bad math.

Maybe it was him.

Chapter 2: Self-Knowledge & Your Money Personality

KIA

Kia was sitting at her kitchen table with her daughter's watercolor painting drying beside her, laptop open, notebook in hand.

She'd just finished Chapter 2 of *SMART Money Makeover* — the one about money personalities.

She felt seen.

First Responder.
Always helping everyone else. Always putting herself last.

"Whew," she whispered.

Chapter 2: Self-Knowledge & Your Money Personality

Growing up, Kia had watched her mom work two jobs to keep the lights on — and still say yes to everybody who asked for help.

Church building fund? Yes.
Cousin's rent? Yes.
Groceries for a friend's friend? Somehow, yes.

And now Kia was doing the same.
Helping her ex pay off his car while her rent was overdue.
Sponsoring someone else's baby shower while her own kid outgrew her sneakers.

It wasn't generosity. It was guilt.

She circled a line from the book:

"Self-sacrifice without boundaries is not noble — it's financial sabotage."

That one cut deep.

But it also felt like freedom.

She flipped to a clean page and wrote:

- I can't help others if I'm drowning.
- I am not selfish for saying no.
- My daughter deserves to see me win.

Then she whispered it to herself, twice, like a prayer:

"I am allowed to put myself first."

Chapter 3: Monetary Awareness

Let's talk about money — not theory, not feelings — just the facts.

This is the chapter where we get honest with ourselves about the numbers. What's coming in. What's going out. What's left over. What's missing. And most importantly, what those numbers *mean*.

Because here's the truth:
You can't change what you won't confront.
And you can't manage what you refuse to measure.

But don't worry — this isn't about judgment. It's about **Monetary Awareness**, the "M" in your SMART Money System. This is where we open our eyes, get real, and begin to take our financial power back.

Clarity is Power

Most people walk around with no real idea of what their financial picture looks like. They might know how much they make (kind of). They might know what their rent or mortgage is (hopefully). But beyond that? It's a blur.

Why? Because avoiding the truth feels safer than facing it.

But that avoidance *costs* you — not just in dollars, but in peace, in options, in confidence.

You don't need to be an accountant or an Excel wizard. You just need a simple system that helps you track what's real — so you can take intentional action.

Chapter 3: Monetary Awareness

Step One: Understand Your Cash Flow

Cash flow is the heartbeat of your financial life.

It's the difference between what's coming in and what's going out on a regular basis. And just like with your actual heartbeat, ignoring irregularities can lead to serious issues.

But this is deeper than dollars.

Knowing your cash flow gives you **margin** — the space between surviving and thriving. That margin is what lets you breathe easier, sleep better, and make decisions from a place of peace instead of panic. It gives you options. It gives you agency.

With positive cash flow, you can save, invest, get ahead, and build. With negative cash flow, you're stuck in survival mode — borrowing from Peter to pay Paul and wondering why it never feels like enough.

If you've ever felt like you can't seem to get ahead no matter how much you earn, chances are you've never truly sat down to measure your cash flow.

Let's fix that.

Here's What to Do:

1. **List Your Net Monthly Income**
   Include everything: job(s), side hustles, child support, business revenue, etc. This is what actually hits your bank account after taxes and deductions.

2. **List Your Monthly Expenses**
   Break them into categories: housing, utilities, food, transportation, debt, subscriptions, etc. Be honest. Don't ballpark.

Chapter 3: Monetary Awareness

3. **Find the Gap**
   Subtract expenses from income. Are you positive, negative, or breaking even? That gap (or lack of one) is where change happens.

🔍 **Coach's Note:**

If you're negative — don't panic. We'll address spending plans and income growth later. Right now, we're just gathering the truth. That's brave. That's progress.

Step Two: Know Your Net Worth

Net worth isn't just for billionaires. It's for *everyone*.

Your net worth is the difference between what you own and what you owe. It's a snapshot of your financial health — not your value as a person.

But here's why it matters: **your net worth shows the long-term trajectory of your financial life.**

If it's negative, that doesn't make you a failure — but it *is* an early warning sign. It means your debt outweighs your assets. If that trend continues over time, it's going to be very difficult to retire, take calculated risks, or build wealth.

You can't retire on cash flow alone. You need assets — things that hold or grow value. A negative net worth is your dashboard light saying, "Let's pay attention here."

We're not fixing that today. You'll learn how to turn things around in upcoming chapters. But awareness is the first step.

Chapter 3: Monetary Awareness

Here's how to figure it out:

- **Assets:** What do you own? This includes cash, savings, investment accounts, retirement funds, property, vehicles, and valuable items.

- **Liabilities:** What do you owe? List all debts — credit cards, student loans, mortgages, car loans, personal loans, etc.

Assets – Liabilities = Net Worth

That number might surprise you. That's okay. What matters is that now, you know. And when you know better, you can do better.

Why This Matters

When you have **Monetary Awareness**, you stop making blind decisions. You stop spending money you don't really have. You stop ignoring debt because it feels too big. And you start building your life on solid ground.

Awareness gives you power. And it gives you *peace*.

Because once the numbers are on paper, they stop chasing you in your head.

What To Watch For (Based On Your Personality)

Let's tie this to your money personality — because how you *feel* about money affects what you do with it.

- **Surfer:** You might avoid tracking because it feels boring or restrictive. Challenge yourself to do it just long enough to prove it's empowering, not punishing.

Chapter 3: Monetary Awareness

- **Soldier**: You probably love tracking — just don't use it as a weapon against yourself or others. Remember, it's a tool, not a scorecard.
- **First Responder**: You may prioritize everyone else's numbers before your own. This is your permission slip to *start with you*.
- **Hunter/Gatherer**: You love chasing goals — but skip the groundwork. Don't guess. Get the real numbers so your ambition is built on a solid foundation.

Quick Exercise: Your Financial Snapshot

Let's keep it simple:

1. Write down your **net monthly income**
2. Write down your **total monthly expenses**
3. Subtract: Income – Expenses = **Monthly cash flow**
4. List your **assets**
5. List your **liabilities**
6. Subtract: Assets – Liabilities = **Net worth**

That's it. This snapshot is your baseline — your launchpad. Don't try to be perfect. Just try to be honest.

And if the numbers are negative, don't stress it. We'll talk about ways to fix that soon enough.

Chapter 3: Monetary Awareness

Coming Up Next:
Now that you know where you stand, it's time to give your money a job. In the next chapter, we'll dive into **Allocated Spending** — building an Intentional Spending Plan that aligns with your values, your lifestyle, and your goals.

You're doing great. Keep going.

Chapter 3: Monetary Awareness

CHAPTER 3 BONUS STORY: The Numbers Don't Lie

ROBERT

Robert sat at his kitchen table with a legal pad, a ballpoint pen, and a strong drink. It was time to "get real," whatever that meant.

He had a stack of unopened mail, a half-used budgeting app on his phone, and about 37 tabs open on his laptop from YouTube guys yelling about passive income and vending machines.

He scribbled some numbers down:

Chapter 3: Monetary Awareness

- Paycheck: $3,700/month
- Rent: $1,200
- Car Note: $650
- Insurance: $215
- Food…?

He paused.

How much had he spent on food last month?
DoorDash. 7-Eleven. Wings. Tacos. Coffee.
The receipts blurred together.

"No way I'm spending *that* much," he muttered.
"I don't even eat like that…"

Then he opened his bank statement.

He did.

After twenty minutes of writing, scratching out, and cussing under his breath, the truth stared back at him: **he was upside down.**

He made too much to be this broke.
But he had more going out than coming in.
No savings. No cushion. No plan.

"How the hell did this happen?" he whispered.

He sat back, hands on his head, eyes burning.
He didn't want to admit it, but here it was:

"I'm living paycheck to paycheck… with a full-time job."

Chapter 3: Monetary Awareness

KIA

Kia was curled up on her couch in a hoodie, laptop open, surrounded by three months' worth of bank statements and a highlighter.

She had just finished reading Chapter 3 — the one that said you can't build anything until you face the truth.

She didn't want to do this.
But she knew she had to.

So she dug in.
She tallied her income:

- Job: $2,800/month (after taxes)

Chapter 3: Monetary Awareness

- Side hustle: $300 (on average each month)

Then her fixed expenses:

- Rent: $1,100
- Childcare: $500
- Transportation: $300
- Groceries: $400
- Other bills: $450

She totaled it all and stared at the number.

"Okay... not as bad as I thought," she said quietly.

She had a **small margin** — about $350 left each month — but she had margin.

For the first time in a long time, she felt... capable.
Not fixed. Not thriving. But not helpless either.

Then she used the book's formula to calculate her **net worth**:

Assets:

- Checking account: $390
- Used car: $2,000
- 403(b): $3,500

Liabilities:

- Credit cards: $2,300
- Student loans: $11,000

Net Worth: **- $7,410**

Chapter 3: Monetary Awareness

Kia winced. But she didn't crumble.
She looked at that negative number and said:

"At least now I know."

She flipped to the next page of the book and underlined a line she loved:

"You can't retire on vibes — you need assets."

Kia smiled.
This wasn't rock bottom. This was her launchpad.

Chapter 3: Monetary Awareness

Chapter 4: Allocated Spending

Giving Every Dollar a Job in YOU, Inc.

Let's pretend for a moment that you're the CEO of a company. And not just any company — **YOU, Inc.**

This company has income, expenses, assets, and debts. It has priorities, goals, risks, and a future to plan for. Sound familiar? That's because whether you realize it or not, you *are* running a business. Your *life* is the business.

And like any good business, your job is simple:

☞ **Make a profit.**

If you don't? YOU, Inc. goes bankrupt!

From Budgeting to Intention

Most people hate the word *budget*. It feels restrictive. Punishing. Like a financial version of a crash diet. That's why I don't use it.

Instead, I talk about an **Intentional Spending Plan** — a living strategy that aligns your money with your values, your lifestyle, and your goals. One that builds in *pleasure* so you don't rebel and burn out. One that reflects *you*.

Intentional Spending isn't about restriction. It's about direction. You're telling your money where to go so you don't have to wonder where it went.

Chapter 4: Allocated Spending

Start with a Look Back

Before you write a single category down, take a good hard look at where your money has *actually* been going.

Pull your bank and credit card statements for the past **90 days**. What patterns do you see? What surprises you? What categories are quietly bleeding you dry?

This isn't about shame — it's about **awareness**.
We can't fix what we won't face. But when we see the truth clearly, we can create change confidently.

The 70/10/10/10 Rule

Once you've gotten honest about your past, it's time to design your future using my **70/10/10/10 Rule**:

- ☑ **Live on no more than 70%** of your net monthly income
- ☑ **Save 10%** (short-term savings)
- ☑ **Invest 10%** (long-term wealth building)
- ☑ **Use 10% for your debt snowball acceleration** (or split between saving/investing if you're debt-free)

This simple framework gives your money purpose, breathing room, and balance. It makes sure you're not just spending to survive — you're building something that lasts.

Chapter 4: Allocated Spending

Know Your Fixed Expenses

Your **fixed living expenses** — the non-negotiables — should fall between **50–60%** of your net monthly income. These include:

- Housing (mortgage or rent)
- Utilities (water, electricity, internet, gas)
- Food (groceries, not takeout)
- Transportation (gas, car payment, public transit)
- Debt obligations (loans, minimum payments)
- Insurance, subscriptions, and any other monthly bills with a due date

If it has a due date, it's a fixed expense. Period.

The 5 Pillars Come First

When life gets tight, or your income isn't consistent, you must prioritize what I call the **5 Pillars**:

1. **Mortgage/Rent** – You need a roof over your head
2. **Utilities** – Light, heat, water — non-negotiables
3. **Food** – Groceries first, eating out second
4. **Transportation** – Car or public transit — you've got to get to work
5. **Clothing** – Especially if you've got growing kids

Chapter 4: Allocated Spending

Until the 5 Pillars are covered, nothing else gets added to the plan. No eating out. No entertainment. No "fun money." You can't have Netflix if you don't have lights.

Variable Income? Create Two Budgets

If your income fluctuates — like in sales, real estate, freelancing, or business — you need **two budgets**:

1. The Basic Budget

This covers your 5 Pillars and absolutely nothing else. Think of it as your "bare minimum survival" plan.

2. The Wish List Budget

Everything else goes here — subscriptions, eating out, fun money, date nights, giving, etc.

Here's how it works: Once your basic budget is covered for the month, go to your wish list and ask:

"If I could only do *one* thing on this list, what would it be?"

That becomes Item #1, so write a '1' next to it.
Then ask again:

"If I could only do *one more* thing, what would it be?"

That becomes item #2, so write a '2' next to it.

Keep going until everything is ranked in order of priority. You only get to spend on wish list items when the money is physically in hand. And if the money isn't there this month? You don't do the thing. No exceptions.

This keeps YOU, Inc. profitable — and alive.

Chapter 4: Allocated Spending

Don't Forget Your Personality

Remember the money personality types from Chapter 2?

- **Surfers**: Build in fun — but give yourself limits. Treats are allowed, but track them.

- **Soldiers**: Budget for pleasure. You're allowed to enjoy your money too.

- **First Responders**: Prioritize self-care. Don't give to others until your 5 Pillars are rock solid.

- **Hunter/Gatherers**: Plan for big goals — but make sure your basic needs are covered first.

You can't create a lasting plan unless it fits *you*. If it's too tight or too boring, you'll rebel. If it's too loose, you'll drift. Balance is key.

If the Math Doesn't Work...

What happens if, after writing your plan, your expenses are higher than your income? Or, what if your ratios are off the guidelines?

You have four options:

1. **Cut some expenses** (especially from your wish list)

2. **Reduce fixed bills** (shop around for insurance, cancel subscriptions, negotiate rates)

3. **Bring in more income** (side hustle, raise, sell stuff, add a new stream)

4. **Do a combo of all three**

Chapter 4: Allocated Spending

Yes, cutting helps — but there's a limit to how much you can cut. There is *no limit* to how much you can earn. Don't just look for what to trim. Look for what you can grow.

So, my advice is leverage a skill or passion and start a side hustle. Teach what you know, bake, make or fix things. Tell, tell, tell everyone what you do and ask, ask, ask for business!

The Goal: A Plan That Feels Like Freedom

You're not meant to live like a monk. You're meant to live with **intention**.

A great spending plan is one that works for your lifestyle, honors your values, supports your goals — and lets you breathe. It should leave room for joy, progress, generosity, and yes, a little fun.

Now, don't expect to create the perfect spending plan the first time out of the gate. It will probably take you 60-90 days to dial in the right numbers. This is a work in progress. It took me a few months to dial it in, but I eventually got it right. You will too.

You're the CEO of YOU, Inc.
Start running it like a business.
A *profitable* one.

Tips For Couples

If you are a couple, there is usually one who is more of a free spirit and one who is more of a numbers person. Let the one who is a numbers person create the actual budget. Then, the free spirit should review it and the two of you should adjust as needed to make both of you happy.

Chapter 4: Allocated Spending

When disagreements arise, remember what your ultimate goal is. If you can agree on that, you can agree on what things will help you get there and what things hinder you from getting there.

If conflict has been the hallmark of your relationship lately, try changing venues. Maybe go out to a nice restaurant and talk there. Pack a picnic lunch and go to the park to do your spending plan.

Neutral places go a long way to defusing the power struggle and create a more relaxed atmosphere where open, honest and calm talk can take place.

Above all, be agreeable. As long as it's not a matter of principle, why not consider compromising to make your mate happy?

And, name calling should never be an option. Stripping someone of their dignity may make you feel powerful in the moment, but words spoken in anger can never be taken back and the damage can last a lifetime.

Both of you need to determine what type of relationship you want to have and what type of future you want to build. Focus on what you want, not on what you don't have or are not getting. Whatever you focus on, you will get more of. So, choose your focus wisely.

You want to win the war. The battles along the way don't matter as much as long as you both win *together*.

Coming Up Next:
Now that your plan is in place, it's time to protect it. In the next chapter, we'll talk about **Ready Cash** — how to build an emergency fund, manage irregular income, and create savings that give you real peace of mind.

You're building something powerful. Keep going.

Chapter 4: Allocated Spending

Chapter 4: Allocated Spending

CHAPTER 4 BONUS STORY: The Plan (or Lack of One)

ROBERT

Robert had a fresh planner from Target and a new pen with gold trim. That was his idea of starting fresh.

He opened a blank page and titled it: "Budget."

Then he stared at it.
And stared some more.
Then he opened TikTok.

A guru said, *"Use cash envelopes and never spend on anything non-essential."*

Chapter 4: Allocated Spending

Another said, *"Treat yourself weekly or your inner child will sabotage you."*

He rolled his eyes, then scribbled down some guesses:

- Rent: $1,200
- Groceries: $250 (that was a lie — he spent double that on takeout)
- Gas: $150
- "Fun": $300
- Extra: ???

He gave up after 15 minutes and wrote:

"Just spend less this month. That's the plan."

Two days later, he impulsively upgraded his phone.

The next week, he overdrafted his checking account after sending his ex $300 to "hold her over."

By the end of the month, he had no idea where his money went.

But he did know this:

"Budgeting is for broke people."
He said it out loud — but even he didn't believe himself anymore.

Chapter 4: Allocated Spending

KIA

Kia printed out her last 90 days of bank statements and sat at her table with a cup of tea and a purpose.

She highlighted every line item. Categorized everything.
The truth hurt — but it also helped.

Then she opened to Chapter 4 and followed Forrest's 70/10/10/10 Rule:

- 70% for living
- 10% to savings
- 10% to investing

Chapter 4: Allocated Spending

- 10% to debt snowball acceleration

She smiled.

"This actually makes sense."

She built her first Intentional Spending Plan:

- Rent & bills fell neatly under 60%
- Food, gas, and essentials covered another 10%
- That left space to finally save — and even set aside a little to treat herself

She had trimmed a little here and there to get to the recommended percentages, but mor importantly calculated how she could double her side-hustle income with just a little extra effort. That brought her under the 70% total of her net monthly income she could afford to spend to live.

She also made a **basic budget** for tight months and a **wish list budget** for better ones.

Her wish list?

- Take her daughter to the zoo
- Get her brakes fixed
- Start a vacation fund

She ranked them. She smiled again.
She felt… in control.

Kia wasn't living large.
But for the first time in a long time, she was living on *purpose*.

Chapter 5: Ready Cash

Why Cash is Still King (Especially When Things Fall Apart)

If there's one thing the COVID pandemic reminded me of, it's this:

Cash is King.

They can shut down your job.
They can shut down your business.
They can shut down your lines of credit.
But they can't shut down **your cash.**

During that season, I saw people with great credit scores get denied when they needed it most. Credit cards got frozen. Lines of credit disappeared overnight. Banks weren't returning calls.

But those who had **cash on hand** — even just a little — slept better. They didn't panic. They didn't slide further into debt. They had **margin**, and that margin gave them peace of mind, confidence, and control.

That's what *Ready Cash* is all about — creating a system of cash reserves that protects you from disaster and keeps **YOU, Inc.** afloat when life gets unpredictable.

Step 1: Build Your Beginner Emergency Fund

Let's start simple.
You don't need to save three months of expenses right away.
You just need to hit a target that *most* emergencies fall under: **$1,000.**

I call this your **Beginner Emergency Fund** — your golden parachute. It's not everything, but it's enough to keep a crisis from becoming a catastrophe.

Chapter 5: Ready Cash

Credit cards can't do that for you. Credit cards can only get you into more debt, which means more stress, which means staying broke.

We started with $1,000 ourselves — and guess what? It handled most of what life threw at us. Broken furnace? Covered. Plumbing disaster? Handled. Car issues? Solved without using plastic.

This fund isn't for fun.
Not for the iPhone upgrade. Not for shoes. Not for playoff tickets.

It's for genuine emergencies. And when you use it? Refill it. Immediately!

You will sleep a little more soundly and walk with a little extra pep in your step as long as you have it.

Can't imagine finding $1,000?

You're not alone. 60% of Americans can't even handle a $400 emergency. But I've seen people hit this goal fast when they get focused and creative. Here are some of the same strategies I shared in my first book and that I used myself:

- Shop around for cheaper car insurance (I saved $1,200 doing this!)
- Cut cable or streaming extras (I did that)
- Brown bag your lunch (Did that too)
- Cook more, eat out less (Yup)
- Sell stuff (yes, maybe even that treadmill-turned-clothes-hanger. I sold my old X-Box, among other things)
- Pick up a side hustle — Uber, photography, gig work, create a course (I did Uber and created a course)
- Adjust your tax withholding to get that monthly refund early (Yep, I did this)

Chapter 5: Ready Cash

- Netflix and chill instead of movie theater splurges (I did lots of that!)

Point is — it's possible. If I did it, you can do it too. **Make it a mission.** Get that $1,000, stash it in a savings account, and protect it like your life depends on it — because sometimes, it just might.

Step 2: Create a Hill & Valley Account

This one's for all my entrepreneurs, commission-based workers, real estate agents, creatives, and anyone with a **variable income**.

You already know the stress of the feast-or-famine cycle. Some months you're flush with cash. Others you're eating ramen and praying for a miracle. I lived this way for years.

Enter the **Hill & Valley Account** — your income-smoothing system. Ta-Da! This discovery changed my life.

Here's how it works:

- In **high-income months**, you add to this account, even if it means trimming some extras.
- In **low-income months**, you draw from it, but this should be only to cover the 5 Pillars.

This way, your lifestyle stays level even if your income doesn't. You don't spiral every slow month. You just breathe, plan, and keep it moving.

This account gives you the stability your paycheck doesn't.

Chapter 5: Ready Cash

Step 3: Build Your Sinking Fund

A sinking fund is **not** for emergencies. It's for expenses you *know* are coming:

- Quarterly tax payments
- Car maintenance
- Insurance premiums
- Back-to-school shopping
- Holiday travel
- That cousin's wedding in Cabo

Most people treat these like surprises — but they're not. You saw them coming. You just didn't plan for them.

So here's the move:

Take the total amount of the upcoming expense and divide it by the number of months until it's due.

That number is what you save each month. When the bill comes, the money's already there — and your emergency fund stays untouched.

For example: Your insurance premium is due in 6 months and it costs $600. $600 divided by 6 months means you would add $100 each month into your Sinking Fund. You would make that calculation and add the required sum for each upcoming expense. Don't forget this line item in your budget.

It's just math. And it's magic!

Chapter 5: Ready Cash

Step 4: Fund Your Dreams with Long-Term Savings

Not every savings goal is for emergencies or bills.

Some are for dreams — big ones.

A new home.
A new car.
A bucket-list vacation.
An opportunity to invest in a business or make a career move.

These aren't "needs" — they're desires. And they're worth planning for.

Treat your **Long-Term Savings** like you would any other goal. Give it a name, give it a timeline, and fund it monthly. You'll be amazed how fast $100/month turns into thousands over time.

Cash Gives You Confidence

Every one of these cash accounts is a tool for breathing easier.

You don't want to be financially fit but emotionally fried.

- Your **Emergency Fund** keeps you out of panic mode.
- Your **Hill & Valley Account** keeps your income steady when it isn't.
- Your **Sinking Fund** makes big expenses feel small.
- Your **Long-Term Savings** brings the future within reach.

This is what **Ready Cash** is all about — *freedom before you're rich.*
Peace before you're perfect.
And the confidence that comes from knowing YOU, Inc. is covered, no matter what.

Chapter 5: Ready Cash

Now, you may be thinking about investing at this point. Be patient. We will get to that later. For now, we need to lay the firm foundation that savings will give you. Let's learn to walk before we run!

Where To Keep Your Cash

You should keep your cash stash in an easy to access location like a no-fee savings or checking account.

I find that online banks generally pay the best rates.

Next come credit unions.

But there are currently some banks out there that pay an above average rate couple with low or no fees.

Wherever you choose to keep it, make sure it is connected to a checking account with a debit card attached to it so you can access it in a pinch, like when you're standing in the auto mechanic's shop.

Coming Up Next:
Let's talk credit and debt. The next chapter is all about **Targeted Credit Use & Your Debt Snowball** — how to use credit intentionally and strategically, not impulsively or emotionally. And how to get debt-free in the most efficient manner possible.

You've got momentum now. Let's keep it going!

Chapter 5: Ready Cash

CHAPTER 5 BONUS STORY: When It Rains

ROBERT

The knock at the door came at 7:13 a.m. sharp.

"Mr. Turner?"

"Yeah?"

"This is your final notice from the electric company. We've sent two previous letters…"

Robert stood there in gym shorts and a t-shirt with one sock on, staring at the yellow slip in the man's hand.

His lights were about to get cut off.

Chapter 5: Ready Cash

"Can I pay it right now?"
"Sure. Balance is $387.19."

Robert pulled out his phone and opened his bank app.
$63.84.

His heart sank. He told the man to wait and called his cousin. No answer. Then his ex. Straight to voicemail.

By noon, his apartment was dark.
No lights. No Wi-Fi. No microwave.

The worst part?

"This wasn't even a real emergency," he muttered.
"I just... didn't plan."

That night, he drove to a gas station to charge his phone.
He stared at the glow of the screen, debating whether to get another payday loan.

He hated himself for even thinking about it.
But it felt like the only option.

Chapter 5: Ready Cash

KIA

Kia's car made a terrible clunk when she turned the ignition.

Then it coughed. Then it died.

She closed her eyes and said a soft, exhausted prayer.

"Please not today."

But she didn't panic.
She didn't cry.
She didn't call her mama in tears like she used to.

Chapter 5: Ready Cash

Instead, she pulled out her phone and transferred $400 from her **emergency fund** to her checking account.

Then she called her mechanic and arranged for a tow.

Two weeks earlier, she'd sold her old tablet and cleared out her closet to fund her **$1,000 starter emergency stash** — just like the book said.

And now?
It was doing exactly what it was designed to do.

Later that day, while waiting on repairs, she re-read the section on **sinking funds** and wrote out new goals:

- $100/month for car maintenance
- $80/month for holiday travel
- $50/month for her daughter's birthday in August

"This is how people stay calm," she realized.
"They don't *hope* it works out. They *plan* for it."

On her next payday, Kia smiled as she sipped her coffee and tapped transfer:
$100 to replenish the emergency fund.

"Murphy's Law met its match."

Chapter 6: Targeted Credit Use & Your Debt Snowball

Paying Off Debt and Using Credit With Purpose

Let me be upfront:

Credit is *not* the enemy.
But using credit **without a plan**? That's how good people end up stuck, stressed, and broke.

Credit cards, car loans, student loans, personal loans, store cards — they can all become traps if you're not intentional. But when you know what you're doing, credit can actually be a powerful tool in your financial strategy.

That's what this chapter is all about:

- Paying off the wrong kinds of debt fast
- Using credit the *right* way going forward

Part 1: Paying Off Debt

Debt doesn't just drain your bank account.
It drains your energy. Your focus. Your peace of mind.
You feel it every time a due date rolls around. Every time you swipe and secretly wonder, "How am I gonna pay for this later?"

Let's stop that cycle — not with shame, but with a plan.

Chapter 6: Targeted Credit Use & Your Debt Snowball

Step 1: List Every Debt

Before you can pay it off, you need to see the full picture. Pull out your credit card statements, loan balances, car notes, medical bills — everything. Everything except for your mortgage. We'll deal with that later.

Create a list with:

- The **name** of the lender
- The **total balance**
- The **minimum payment**
- The **interest rate** (just for awareness — we're not using it to decide payoff order)

We're not judging it. We're just acknowledging it. And that's powerful.

Step 2: Use the Debt Snowball Method (Because Math Isn't the Problem)

People love to get fancy with what they call the **avalanche method**, claiming it saves more on interest because you tackle the highest-interest debt first.

Let me tell you something:

If debt were a math problem, you wouldn't be in debt.

You didn't get here because you're bad at math.
You got here — just like I did — because you made a bunch of emotional, impulsive decisions. You bought things to feel better. You swiped a card to keep up appearances. You financed things you couldn't afford to prove something, or to escape something.

Chapter 6: Targeted Credit Use & Your Debt Snowball

Debt is emotional.
And if you try to fight emotion with a calculator, you will *lose* every time.

Here's what works much better instead: the **Debt Snowball** method.

This is how it goes:

1. **List your debts** from smallest balance to largest.

2. **Make minimum payments** on all of them.

3. Take every extra dollar you can squeeze from your spending plan, including the 10% we allocated to the debt snowball, and throw it at the **smallest** debt first.

4. Once that's paid off, roll everything you were paying on that into the next smallest.

5. Keep going until you've knocked out every last one.

Why? Because it creates **quick wins**.
It builds **momentum**.
It gives you **visible progress** that motivates you to keep going.

You will wear yourself out trying to tackle a massive, high-interest debt right out of the gate. The math might make sense on paper, but you'll burn out emotionally — and then give up.

I've used the debt snowball method myself.
So have my clients.
And millions of other people.

It works.
Because it speaks to the part of you that needs hope. That needs a win. That needs to feel like this mountain is climbable.

The debt avalanche might make sense on paper — but in real life?

Chapter 6: Targeted Credit Use & Your Debt Snowball

It doesn't belong anywhere near this plan.

We're not here for spreadsheets.
We're here for results.

> ***Pro Tip**: If funds are tight and you don't have enough to go around, leave out "zombie debt." These are old debts where the creditor may not have contacted you in years. My advice here is let sleeping dogs lie. You can deal with them later. Right now, focus your attention on active debts only. So, don't poke the bear!*

Step 3: Keep Paying Even When It Hurts

There will be months when it feels slow. Like you're barely making a dent. Like it's not working.

But here's the truth:
Every payment is progress.
Every dollar you redirect toward debt is a step closer to freedom.

You're not just paying off credit cards.
You're reclaiming your options.
You're buying back your peace of mind.

When It's A Good Idea To Pause Your Debt Snowball

It would be nice if life cooperated all the time and we never ran into the unexpected. But, the reality is that life will life on you from time to time, because that's just what it does. So here are some times when you will need to pause your debt snowball and pile up cash instead:

- Pregnancy- I pray that your pregnancy goes without a hitch, but sometimes there are complications. Difficulties can arise and the woman may have to quit work earlier than expected and go on bed rest. Other post-delivery problems may require more cash to

Chapter 6: Targeted Credit Use & Your Debt Snowball

address a delay in return to work or medical bills. A pile of cash will be a handy resource to call on when these things happen.
- An adverse medical diagnosis- Medical bills can add up quickly so when faced with an uncertain treatment course and the costs connected to it, it would be best to pause your debt snowball and pile up cash instead.
- Work uncertainty- If there are serious signs that your paycheck might end due to layoffs, pay cuts or strike, this is an appropriate time to pile up cash.

In each of these instances, if things go better than expected, you can always un-pause your debt snowball and throw all that sweet cash at it, picking up right where you left off.

When Bankruptcy Seems To Be The Only Option

When your back is against the wall and creditors seem to be coming from all directions, when they seem to want your firstborn and a kidney, bankruptcy can seem like the only way out.

I know how that feels because I filed bankruptcy at the age of 25. It didn't work for me and let me tell you why.

Yes, I got a temporary reprieve from the creditors, but that's all it was, temporary. Because I didn't address the underlying behavioral problems that caused me to go deep in debt in the first place, I did it again a few years later.

The fact is that over 40% of people who file Chapter 7 (total discharge of all debts) bankruptcy end up doing it again! The simple reason for that is that we who chose that route took the easy way out and didn't really do the hard work of fixing ourselves and our bad habits.

Chapter 6: Targeted Credit Use & Your Debt Snowball

Until you dig deep, figure out why you keep going into debt and being unable to repay what you owe, you are bound to do it again because it's just too easy for it to happen. There will always be bottom-feeding creditors eager to lend to a recovering "debtaholic."

So, when I got into a debt jam again, I said no to bankruptcy. I promised myself I would never file again and I am happy to say I kept that promise. From that commitment came many of the principles you see in this book, and they worked for me then and my clients today.

Another great reason not to file bankruptcy is that it may have little to no effect on your outstanding debt obligations.

The following debts cannot be discharged in bankruptcy:

- Student loans
- Tax obligations
- Judgements
- Child support
- Debts from fraud, theft or embezzlement
- Court-ordered fines and penalties
- Debts from divorce settlements

Since these debts make up a major chunk of common debt out there, you may file only to suffer all the adverse effects of the process without gaining much in the way of financial freedom.

And... if you want to keep your car, etc., you have to file Chapter 13 or 11, which is an arrangement to reorganize your finances and repay what you owe. And, you can do that with your individual creditors anyway!

So, no, I do not endorse bankruptcy. Having been through the fire I can say that the best option is to repay every dime you owe. That will build character and leave a mark that will create lasting change in the way you manage your money and credit.

Chapter 6: Targeted Credit Use & Your Debt Snowball

Part 2: Using Credit Wisely

Now let's flip the script.

Because once your toxic debt is gone — or even while you're working on it — it's time to rethink what credit is *for*.

Credit should serve your strategy. Not your impulses.

Good Credit Use vs. Bad Credit Use

Let's break it down.

Bad Credit Use:

- Swiping to buy things you can't afford
- Treating credit like income
- Making minimum payments and carrying balances
- Using "buy now, pay later" to justify emotional purchases

Chapter 6: Targeted Credit Use & Your Debt Snowball

Good Credit Use:

- Leveraging low-interest financing for *appreciating* assets (home, education, business equipment)
- Keeping utilization low (below 30%) to build your credit score
- Paying off full balances every month
- Earning rewards without paying interest

Credit is a **tool**, not a paycheck. You should be using it with intention, not desperation.

Ask This Before You Use Credit

Every time you reach for that card, ask:

"Is this a tool I'm leveraging — or a trap I'm setting?"

If the answer feels fuzzy, **pause**.
You're the **CEO** of **YOU, Inc.** Would your business survive if it ran up credit for things it couldn't afford and made minimum payments for life?

Nope.
And neither will you.

When Credit Makes Sense

Here's when using credit might actually be wise:

- Starting a business with a clear, realistic revenue plan
- Buying a home or real estate that appreciates over time
- Financing a car within your budget that enables income

Chapter 6: Targeted Credit Use & Your Debt Snowball

- Building or rebuilding credit with a secured card you pay off monthly

Again — the key word is **intention**.

You're not using credit because you're out of options.
You're using it because it supports your long-term goals.

Let Credit Work *For* You, Not Against You

One of the most powerful shifts you can make is to stop letting credit control you — and start using it with *strategy*.

Pay off what's hurting you.
Avoid what tempts you.
Use what helps you.
And always, always act from **wisdom**, not impulse.

You don't need a perfect score.
You need a credit strategy that aligns with your future.

Note: You will find some great tips on rebuilding your credit in the bonus section.

Coming Up Next:
Now that your SMART system is complete, it's time to bring it all together. In the next chapter, we'll walk through your **30-Day SMART Money Makeover Challenge** — a practical way to put everything you've learned into motion.

You're almost there. Let's finish strong.

Chapter 6: Targeted Credit Use & Your Debt Snowball

Chapter 6: Targeted Credit Use & Your Debt Snowball

CHAPTER 6 BONUS STORY: Credit Games

ROBERT

Robert sat in his car outside the payday loan place for a full ten minutes before going in.

This was supposed to be the last time.

The clerk barely looked up.

"Same amount as last time?"
"Yeah."
"We'll need a check for $575, post-dated to the 15th."

Chapter 6: Targeted Credit Use & Your Debt Snowball

He nodded, his stomach turning.

Back home, he stared at his spreadsheet — the one he downloaded but hadn't filled out. Five credit cards. Two loans. A car note. Everything was maxed or late.

He opened another tab: *Debt Avalanche vs. Debt Snowball*
Too many opinions. Too much jargon.

He closed it.
His head hurt. His pride hurt more.

That night, he got another "friendly reminder" email about a $24,000 balance on a card with a 29% interest rate.

He poured himself a drink and stared at the screen.

"Maybe if I pick up a second job…"

But deep down, he knew it wasn't an income problem.
It was a **behavior** problem.

He kept trying to out-hustle his spending instead of changing it.

And credit?
It had gone from tool to trap.

Chapter 6: Targeted Credit Use & Your Debt Snowball

KIA

Kia laid out her debts like soldiers on a battlefield. Each one listed in her notebook:

1. Visa – $327
2. Target – $582
3. Capital One – $1,040
4. Student Loans – $11,000

She made the **minimum payments** on all but the first. That one? She attacked.

77

Chapter 6: Targeted Credit Use & Your Debt Snowball

She used the 10% debt piece of her 70/10/10/10 plan and added $100 from a tutoring side gig.

The book said to ignore interest rates for now — just go for the **smallest balance first**.

"I need quick wins," she reminded herself.
"I need to feel like I'm getting somewhere."

One month later, that first card was gone. She cut it up.
Not out of anger — but out of *peace*.

Then she rolled that payment into the next card.

"This is what momentum feels like," she whispered.

When her coworker tried to talk her into getting a store card "for the discount," she smiled and said no.

Not because she was broke.
But because she had **clarity**.

Credit wasn't the enemy anymore.
She was just finally using it *on purpose*.

Chapter 7: The 30-Day SMART Money Makeover Challenge

Put the Plan in Motion, One Step at a Time

You've learned the system. You've faced the truth. You've felt the shift. Now it's time to put it all into motion.

This is your 30-Day SMART Money Makeover Challenge.

The goal? Build consistency. Get some wins. And prove to yourself that financial transformation doesn't have to be complicated — it just has to be *intentional*.

This is where we move from theory to traction. And the best part? You don't have to do it all at once. This challenge breaks your SMART system into **one pillar per week**, with clear steps, reflection prompts, and habits to build on. Get the companion Challenge PDF at:

https://intentionalmoneysolutions.com/resources/

Week 1: Self-Knowledge – *Know Thyself, Know Your Flow*

This week is all about internal awareness — your beliefs, patterns, and personality.

Your Focus:

- Review your Money Personality type (from Chapter 2)
- Journal about your money story: What messages did you pick up growing up?
- Identify one belief you want to rewrite and what you'll replace it with

Chapter 7: The 30-Day SMART Money Makeover Challenge

- Share your insights with a trusted friend, coach, or partner (if you're brave!)

Small Win Goal:

Say *no* to one spending decision this week that doesn't align with the person you're becoming.

Week 2: Monetary Awareness – *Measure to Master*

Time to check in with your numbers and get brutally honest (without shame).

Your Focus:

- Review your cash flow and net worth snapshot (Chapter 3)
- Log every dollar you spend this week — no skipping
- Identify at least **two areas** where money is leaking (subscriptions, eating out, etc.)
- Plug one of those leaks — cut it, pause it, or replace it with a lower-cost version

Small Win Goal:

Find at least **$100 in savings** this week — through cutting or renegotiating.

Week 3: Allocated Spending – *Give Your Money a Job*

Here's where you take control. Time to build your **Intentional Spending Plan** and make it reflect YOU, Inc.

Your Focus:

Chapter 7: The 30-Day SMART Money Makeover Challenge

- Design your 70/10/10/10 plan
- Prioritize the 5 Pillars
- Review the past 90 days and create your plan based on *actual* spending
- If you're on variable income, set up your basic and wish list budgets
- Pick one thing from your wish list to delay or skip this month — practice discipline

Small Win Goal:

Finalize and *live by* your Intentional Spending Plan for at least 7 days.

Week 4: Ready Cash & Targeted Credit Use – *Protect the Plan, Then Power It*

This final week brings it all together — saving for the unexpected, and handling credit with strategy.

Your Focus:

- Fund or restart your **$1,000 Emergency Fund**
- Set up a **Hill & Valley Account** (if variable income applies to you)
- Choose one future bill to start a **sinking fund** for (use the division method)
- Create a **debt snowball list** and start your first extra payment
- Cut up or hide one credit card you've been using emotionally or irresponsibly

Chapter 7: The 30-Day SMART Money Makeover Challenge

Small Win Goal:

Save at least **$250** between your emergency, sinking, or long-term accounts by week's end (or more if you're able!).

Wrap-Up: What Changed in 30 Days?

By now, you've:

- Learned what drives your decisions
- Faced your financial truth
- Designed a plan with your values at the center
- Created cushion, clarity, and control
- Taken real steps toward eliminating debt

This is more than a challenge — it's a *preview* of your new normal.

As a thank you for purchasing this book, you can download a free, step-by-step Challenge Worksheet. The bonus section tells you how to get it.

Final Reflection Questions:

- What's one thing I'm proud of accomplishing this month?
- Where did I surprise myself?
- What's still challenging — and what support do I need to overcome it?
- Who can I share my progress with to stay accountable?

Chapter 7: The 30-Day SMART Money Makeover Challenge

CHAPTER 7 BONUS STORY: All In

ROBERT

Robert stared at his vision board.

It had pictures of cars, condos, stacks of cash, and a private jet he couldn't spell the name of. He watched another video titled *"How to 10X Your Life in 30 Days."*

He'd seen it all before.
None of it stuck.

He didn't want another pep talk. He wanted results.
But the truth?

Chapter 7: The 30-Day SMART Money Makeover Challenge

He still hadn't done the basics.

No emergency fund.
No plan.
No budget.
No debt strategy.

He told himself he was "waiting for the right time."
Waiting for a bigger paycheck.
Waiting to get his taxes back.
Waiting until he felt more motivated.

In the meantime, his spending was still emotional.
His bills were still late.
And his credit score… was still in the 500s.

He picked up his journal, flipped to an empty page, and stared.

Then he put it back down.

"I'll start Monday," he mumbled.

But deep down, he knew:

Monday never comes for people who won't move.

Chapter 7: The 30-Day SMART Money Makeover Challenge

KIA

Kia taped a sticky note to her mirror.

"Day 1. I can do hard things."

She was doing the 30-Day SMART Challenge — not just reading it, but actually *living* it.

Week 1, she revisited her money story.
She wrote a letter to her younger self and forgave the version of her that didn't know better.

Week 2, she tracked every dollar that left her account.
No shame. Just truth.

Chapter 7: The 30-Day SMART Money Makeover Challenge

Week 3, she reworked her Intentional Spending Plan to include a small "fun" fund.
She bought herself a used book and a candle. And it felt *good*.

Week 4, she sent an extra $75 toward her second credit card.
It wasn't much — but it was *something*.

Each step gave her back a little more confidence.
A little more control.
A little more joy.

"This isn't just a challenge," she wrote in her journal.
"This is who I'm becoming."

By Day 30, she had saved $412, paid off another card, and started sleeping through the night again.

Not because she was rich.
But because she was no longer *running from her money*.

She was walking *with it*.

Chapter 8: High Walls, Wide Moat

How Insurance Protects What You've Built

There's a reason castles were built with **high walls** and a **wide moat**: To keep danger out and protect what mattered most inside.

That's exactly what the right insurance does for you and your family.
It doesn't build your wealth. But it **preserves** it.
It's not about getting rich — it's about making sure one accident, one illness, or one disaster doesn't wipe out everything you've worked so hard to build.

Why Insurance Matters

Some people don't like the idea of insurance. It feels like a waste — paying for something you *might* never need.

But here's the reality:

If something goes wrong, and you don't have it, you're not just in trouble — you're broke.

And if you're thinking, "I'll just self-insure," let me tell you: that's a great theory until life happens.

If you become critically ill, your loved ones may empty every account they have just trying to keep you alive. You might survive… but broke. Or you might die — and leave your family not only grieving, but scrambling. Either way, *nobody wins*.

Insurance is **your financial moat**.
And unlike your investments or bank accounts, insurance payouts are:

- **Tax-free**

Chapter 8: High Walls, Wide Moat

- **Protected from creditors**
- **Unattachable in lawsuits or bankruptcy**

That's peace of mind on a whole different level.

The Big 5: Life, Health, Long-Term Care, Disability, and Property & Casualty

Let's break this down into practical, understandable parts. You don't need to be a financial advisor — you just need a working knowledge so you can make wise decisions.

---

1. Life Insurance: Protect the People You Love

There are three major types of life insurance:

- **Term**
- **Whole Life**
- **Universal/Variable Life**

You already know my stance here:

✗ All cash value? Too expensive.
✗ Term-only and invest the rest? Risky.
☑ Balanced approach? Smart and sustainable.

Here's the quick and clear breakdown:

Term Life

- Inexpensive, high coverage.
- Best for temporary needs — mortgage, raising children, etc.

Chapter 8: High Walls, Wide Moat

- **Downside:** It expires. And if you're in poor health when it does, you may not be insurable again. Don't assume you'll "invest the rest" and be set. Many don't.

If you get term, make sure it's **level term** and has a **conversion option** in case your health changes.

Whole Life

- Lasts your entire life.
- Premiums don't change.
- Builds cash value you can **borrow** from or use in emergencies.
- Helps **guarantee** your insurability and ensure money is there — no matter when you go.

I've seen clients use their cash value to expand businesses, avoid debt, and create stability when banks weren't lending. It's not an investment. It's protection. View it that way.

Universal/Variable Life

- Hybrid of term and whole.
- Tied to market performance.
- If returns dip, **you** have to make up the difference — or the policy collapses.

My advice: Stay away from this particular product. I've seen people blindsided when their premiums spiked and their policies lapsed. If you want to invest in the market, do it **outside** of your insurance.

Pro Tip: When it comes to picking your life insurance mix, beware the person who wants to sell you term and get you to "self-insure" by investing the rest. They will tell you this is a "sophisticated" approach, or

Chapter 8: High Walls, Wide Moat

some other such language. This is but one of many reasons why I don't like Primerica and their copycats.

Let me give you some things to think about:

Some experts will advise you to only take out term policies and never take whole life, which they consider a "bad investment." They say take the money you save and invest it in the stock market so you can self-insure.

I say to them firstly, insurance is NOT an investment. It's insurance, so don't expect it to act like anything other than what it is. It's there to protect your family in the event you die, not provide brisk investment returns. And what if the market takes a dive just before you die? I don't really need to explain that part, do I?

Secondly, self-insuring only works when a person does not incur an extended illness that leads to full-time nursing care or death. All that "self-insurance" money can be depleted in the run up to death in medical expenses.

And if you cannot afford the several hundred thousand dollars that nursing home care can cost nowadays, the state will require you to be destitute before they will pick up your care under Medicaid. That means you have to be declared legally broke, which leaves your family with NOTHING.

Thirdly, self-insurance in whatever form you leave it in, is taxable as part of the estate of the deceased and attachable by creditors. Insurance proceeds are exempt from taxation and is not attachable by any creditor, so the money will make it to your survivors completely intact.

So, while term is a very wise choice as *part* of any insurance portfolio, it is *not* the be all and end all of life insurance. So, reflect on those points before you let someone ram term-only down your throat.

And if you do purchase term, only go with level term. That locks your rate in at a level amount for the life of the policy.

Chapter 8: High Walls, Wide Moat

And make sure you have a conversion option agreeable to you so you have the option to convert all or part of it to whole life if you choose.

Exception: You are not able to get insurance at all or in the amounts you need due to health reasons. Then, you will have no other choice but to look for ways to self-insure for the benefit of your dependents.

---

2. Health Insurance: One Medical Bill Can Break You

Healthcare in the U.S. is expensive. That's just a fact. Even one hospital stay can wipe out your savings.

If your job offers insurance — take it.
If not, explore options like:

- **Marketplace plans**
- **High-deductible plans + Healthcare Savings Account (HAS)**
- **Short-term gap coverage**

Also consider:

- **Critical illness insurance** (lump sum if diagnosed with cancer, heart attack, etc.)
- **Medical savings accounts** (pre-tax savings for medical expenses)

You may not use it every year. But when you need it? You'll thank God it's there.

Pro Tip: HSA's, unlike Medical Savings Accounts, grow in value from year to year, similar to a 401k, if not used and can even be used in retirement for medical care! Talk to your insurance pro about the details.

Chapter 8: High Walls, Wide Moat

Chapter 8: High Walls, Wide Moat

3. Long-Term Care Insurance: Dignity in Old Age

People are living longer. And with that comes the very real possibility of needing long-term care — whether in a nursing home or with a full-time home health aide.

According to Genworth, the average cost of a semi-private room in a nursing home is over **$120,000/year** in many states.

And here's the kicker:
To qualify for state-paid care, you must be **legally broke**. Medicaid forces you to liquidate your assets — leaving your family with *nothing*.

That's why long-term care insurance matters. It protects:

- **Your savings**
- **Your estate**
- **Your independence**

The best time to get it? **Your 40s.** It's more affordable and easier to qualify for earlier in life. Be sure to get one with a **cost-of-living increase rider**, so your benefits keep pace with future expenses.

---

4. Disability Insurance: Your Income Is an Asset

If you couldn't work for 6 months, how would you pay your bills?

That's what **disability insurance** is for. If you're employed, your job may offer some coverage. But read the fine print — many workplace policies **don't cover injuries off the job.**

If you're self-employed or commission-based, you absolutely need your own policy.

Chapter 8: High Walls, Wide Moat

Remember:

- Pregnancy is a top reason women need coverage.
- Sports injuries or even accidents at home can knock you out of commission.

Your paycheck is your engine. Don't leave it unprotected.

---

5. Property & Casualty: Your Stuff (and Lawsuits) Need Coverage Too

This category covers:

- **Auto insurance** — liability, collision, comprehensive
- **Homeowners/renters insurance** — for your house or stuff
- **Umbrella insurance** — for lawsuits that exceed standard policy limits

Pro Tips:

- Renters: Your landlord's insurance doesn't cover **your** stuff.
- Homeowners: Make sure you have a **replacement value** policy.
- Vehicles: Re-evaluate your auto policy yearly, especially for older cars, to make sure the comprehensive part still makes sense and to make sure you are getting the best rates.
- Umbrella: Look at getting this once your net worth surpasses $1,000,000.

This is about protecting your lifestyle and shielding yourself from financial ruin after accidents, fires, floods, or even lawsuits.

Chapter 8: High Walls, Wide Moat

How Much Coverage Do You Need?

This depends on:

- Your income (and how many years you'd want to replace it)
- Your debts (like mortgage, car, credit cards)
- Dependents and college plans
- Monthly expenses
- Final expenses and burial wishes

Pro Tip: Don't just pick a round number.
Have this discussion with a **trusted** insurance professional who won't push a product but will tailor a plan to your needs.

The main thing for you to ask is do you want a stream of income to be generated by this lump sum of cash or, do you mean for it to be spent at the discretion of the beneficiary?

In Summary: Build Your Wall. Fill Your Moat.

When you finish this chapter, you should have or be getting ASAP:

- A combination of **term and whole life** insurance
- Health coverage (with gap protection if needed)
- A long-term care policy or plan to get one
- Disability protection
- Property/casualty coverage (auto, home, renters, umbrella)

That's your high wall. That's your wide moat.

Chapter 8: High Walls, Wide Moat

Now you can sleep better at night, knowing that if the unthinkable happens — you've got backup. You've got a plan. You've got protection.

Coming Up Next:
We're done playing defense.
In the next chapter, we're going on offense.
Let's talk about how to **grow** your money, avoid gimmicks, and invest with confidence — without the hype.

Chapter 8: High Walls, Wide Moat

CHAPTER 8 BONUS STORY: The Shift

ROBERT

Robert sat in the back of his favorite bar, nursing a drink he shouldn't have bought, scrolling through Instagram reels of people "making it."

New cars. New houses. Beach photos with inspirational captions. He laughed — but it didn't feel funny.

He was stuck.
Still in debt. Still ducking calls. Still telling himself, *"Next month."*

He had read just enough books and watched just enough videos to sound like he knew what he was doing — but not enough to *change*.

Chapter 8: High Walls, Wide Moat

"I'm not broke," he told a friend the week before.
"I'm just in transition."

But the truth?

He was in denial.

The same habits. The same excuses. The same stress.

And deep down, he was tired of himself.
Tired of saying he'd change but never following through.

That night, he got home, looked around his apartment, and whispered:

"Is this it?"

No plan. No growth. No peace.

He wasn't in transition.
He was in a loop.

And until something changed **inside**, nothing was going to change on the outside.

Chapter 8: High Walls, Wide Moat

KIA

Kia stood in her tiny kitchen, holding her daughter on her hip, stirring a pot of spaghetti.

The bills were paid.
Groceries were stocked.
Insurance was in place in case of the unthinkable, so that her child would be well-cared for.
And for the first time in years, she had $750 above and beyond her emergency fund in savings — and it hadn't come from a miracle. It came from *discipline*.

She had stopped calling herself "bad with money."

Chapter 8: High Walls, Wide Moat

She started calling herself **a builder.**

And her decisions started following that identity.

She didn't take shortcuts.
She didn't fall for hype.
She made peace with slow progress — and it changed everything.

At night, instead of lying awake with anxiety, she read books on generational wealth. She journaled about the legacy she wanted to leave.

She caught herself smiling for no reason sometimes.
Because it wasn't just her budget that changed — it was her **belief** about what was possible.

Her old life wasn't calling anymore.
And if it did? She wasn't answering.

"This is who I am now," she whispered.

A woman with a plan.
A woman with peace.
A woman who knows her worth — and now builds wealth to match it.

Chapter 9: Investing Without the Hype
Simple Strategies for Building Real Wealth on Your Terms

Let me say this right out the gate:

You cannot count on Social Security alone.
You need a retirement plan — and not the kind that depends on someone else's promise.

Whether you're a W2 employee, 1099 contractor, or business owner, you've got to make peace with one truth: **nobody is coming to save you.** But the good news? You can save yourself — if you invest wisely, consistently, and with intention.

This chapter is your investing **primer** — not a deep dive, but a strong foundation. We'll keep it simple, clear, and hype-free.

Investing Isn't Complicated — It's Just Sold That Way

There's a whole industry built around making you feel too stupid to manage your own money.

The truth?

You don't need to be a genius.
You don't need a finance degree.
You just need a long-term plan, patience, and the ability to ignore noise.

Let's start with what I *don't* recommend.

What NOT to Do

✘ **Don't Day Trade**

Chapter 9: Investing Without the Hype

Statistically, over **95% of day traders lose money** — and the longer they do it, the worse their performance gets. You're not going to beat the market with TikTok tips and Reddit hype.

Day trading isn't a wealth-building strategy. It's a **gamble**, and the house almost always wins.

✖ Don't Buy Individual Stocks

Buying single stocks is like putting all your chips on one number at the roulette table.

If you want to invest in Apple, Google, or Tesla — fine. But do it inside of a **fund**, not on your own. You're not Warren Buffett, and even *he* spreads out risk.

✖ Don't Chase What's Hot

If your barbershop is talking about crypto, it's probably too late. If your Uber driver is hyping NFTs, you missed the wave.

Jumping in and out of "trendy" investments is how regular people lose money — fast.

What TO Do: Buy and Hold, Long-Term

Wealth isn't built by chasing highs.
It's built by **owning quality assets**, contributing consistently, and **holding them** over time.

The kind of investing I teach is boring on purpose.
It's dependable. Scalable. And it works.

The Vehicles I use: Index Funds and Mutual Funds

Chapter 9: Investing Without the Hype

✅ Index Funds

These track a broad market index — like the S&P 500 or Total Market — and spread your money across **hundreds of companies**.

- **Low fees**
- **No guessing**
- **Set it and forget it**

Great for:

- Retirement accounts
- College savings
- General long-term investing

I use index funds because they allow me to participate in the market as a whole and they don't stress me out when one stock dips. I don't have the mental bandwidth to spend worrying about that!

✅ Mutual Funds

Actively managed (with a real person making decisions), mutual funds can be great — but fees are usually higher.

Tip: If you go the mutual fund route, **make sure you understand the fees and track record**. If the fund isn't consistently beating its benchmark, it's not worth the extra cost. And a 1% fee ain't really 1%! It compounds over time and can end up costing you hundreds of thousands of dollars.

Investing by Employment Type

🔖 If You're a W2 Employee:

Chapter 9: Investing Without the Hype

- Start with your company's **401(k)**, especially if they offer a match. At least take advantage of the percentage they will match. That's free money!

- Open a **Roth IRA** if you qualify — contributions go in after-tax, but grow and withdraw *tax-free*. I love Roths because you get taxed at today's tax rate, and not at tomorrow's, then it grows tax free! And if you look at the direction the country is going in, do you think taxes will be higher or lower by the time you retire? I'd rather pay today's tax rate, thank you.

- Once those are maxed, look into a **taxable brokerage account** to keep investing.

If You're 1099 / Self-Employed:

- Open a **SEP IRA** or **Solo 401(k)** — these let you contribute way more than a traditional IRA.

- Consider using a **Roth IRA** too, depending on your income.

- Use business profits to fund **taxable brokerage accounts** for additional growth.

If You Own a Business:

- Build retirement into your **profit plan** — not just your expense sheet.

- Offer retirement plans to employees (if applicable) — this can help with taxes and retention.

- Don't reinvest 100% back into the business. Diversify with outside investments.

Chapter 9: Investing Without the Hype

How to Vet a Financial Advisor

Don't just pick the first person with a fancy business card.

☑ **Interview at least two or three advisors.**

Ask real questions. Get recommendations — but from friends who are actually *doing well*. Broke friends give broke advice.

☑ **Do a background check.**

Use FINRA.org to look up any complaints, suspensions, or red flags. If someone has a shady past, it will show up there.

☑ **Assemble a team.**

You're not just looking for an "advisor" — you want an **advisory team**:

- A CPA or tax expert
- An attorney (especially for estate planning)
- An insurance professional
- A real estate pro
- And your registered investment advisor

Each brings something different to the table. Ask them questions, especially when you don't know the answers. There are no dumb questions.

My father had a wise saying: *"If you don't have brains, buy 'em!"*

But here's the key:

Seek their input, but never give up your decision-making power.

Too many celebrities handed everything over to a "trusted advisor"… and lost everything. That won't be you.

Chapter 9: Investing Without the Hype

Avoid the "Just 1%" Trap

That tiny 1% portfolio management fee doesn't sound like much — until you run the numbers. Over decades, that "small fee" can compound and cost you **hundreds of thousands of dollars**.

Use online calculators to run the math. That 1% could be the difference between a modest retirement and a wealthy one.

Other Rules of the Road

Let's hit some quick wisdom from the trenches:

- **Age-appropriate risk:** Younger? You can take more risk. Older? Time to be more conservative.

- **Net-worth-appropriate investing:** Don't buy "champagne stocks" on a "malt liquor" budget.

- **Avoid hot tips like the plague:** They're either garbage or illegal.

- **Understand what you're investing in:** If your advisor can't explain it clearly, *walk away*.

- **If writing the check makes you sick, don't do it:** No investment should feel like a panic attack. Trust your gut.

Want to Help Your Kids? Start Now.

College isn't cheap. But there are **tax-advantaged ways** to start early.

Chapter 9: Investing Without the Hype

🎓 529 Plans

- Tax-free growth and tax-free withdrawals (for qualified education expenses)
- Some states offer tax deductions for contributions
- Can be transferred to another child if unused

🎓 Coverdell Education Savings Accounts (ESA)

- Also grows tax-free, but with lower contribution limits
- Can be used for private K-12 in addition to college

🎓 UTMA/UGMA Custodial Accounts

- Not tax-advantaged like the others, but allows you to gift money for future use
- Becomes the child's asset at age of majority — so use with care

Don't try to fund everything — even small, consistent contributions can make a **huge** difference later.

Final Word: Real Wealth Takes Time

The market goes up. The market goes down.
Ignore the noise. Stick to your strategy.

"Time in the market beats timing the market — every time."

If you stay the course, automate your investments, and live below your means, wealth is not a matter of *if* — it's a matter of *when*.

You've worked hard to protect what you've built.
Now it's time to grow it — with wisdom, patience, and peace of mind.

Chapter 9: Investing Without the Hype

What's Next?

The SMART system isn't just for 30 days — it's for life. But now, you've got proof that it *works for you*.

In the next (and final) chapter, we'll talk about how to **become the new version of yourself** — the one who doesn't just think differently about money, but *lives differently* every day.

You're not just making over your money.

You're making over your life.

Let's finish strong.

Chapter 9: Investing Without the Hype

CHAPTER 9 BONUS STORY: Transitions

(One Year Later...)

ROBERT

Robert finally hit rock bottom six months after that night in the bar.

Another maxed card.
Another argument with his landlord.
Another job interview blown because his car wouldn't start.

He eventually stopped trying to hack the system and admitted what he had avoided for years:

Chapter 9: Investing Without the Hype

He needed help.

It was humbling.
Uncomfortable.
But necessary.

He picked up *SMART Money Makeover* after hearing about it from a coworker who used to be worse off than him. She couldn't stop singing its praises.
He didn't expect much — but, page by page, something started to shift.

He saw himself in the stories.
He stopped pretending.
He stopped scrolling.
And started *showing up*.

He built his beginner emergency fund.
Paid off one credit card.
Got on a plan that made sense — for him.

He's not debt-free yet.
But he's not drowning anymore.

And for the first time in years, he feels **hope** instead of pressure.

Chapter 9: Investing Without the Hype

KIA

Kia's kitchen is still small.

But now it smells like fresh basil from the window garden she started last fall.

She's six credit cards down, one to go.

Her emergency fund has three months of living expenses.

Her daughter just started gymnastics — paid in full, no stress.

Chapter 9: Investing Without the Hype

She started a small coaching group with two other single moms to help them walk through *SMART Money Makeover* together. It's not official. No website. Just real women, real stories, and real change.

She's no longer just surviving.
She's thriving — and teaching others to do the same.

She's still watching her dollars closely.
But now, she watches them with **intentionality**.

She's constantly reading and learning more about money and investments.

Life for her and her child is good!

She's building a life she doesn't want to escape from — one choice at a time.

Chapter 10: Becoming the New You

You're not just making over your money. You're making over your life.

You made it.

Not just to the end of a book — but to the beginning of a **whole new version of yourself**.
This isn't just about money anymore.
It's about *you* — the version of you that makes decisions from peace, not panic… from purpose, not pressure.

But before we celebrate, let's get real:

This isn't the end of your journey.
It's the *launch point*.

Because even after everything you've learned, you're still going to have moments of:

- Doubt
- Frustration
- Setbacks
- Unexpected expenses
- Emotional spending triggers
- Family members who *still* don't get it

And in those moments, it's easy to feel like nothing has changed.

But here's the truth:

Chapter 10: Becoming the New You

You have changed.
And you *can't unlearn* what you now know.

🧠 Who You Were vs. Who You Are Becoming

Old You:

- Avoided the numbers
- Lived check to check
- Tried to fix emotional pain with spending
- Reacted instead of planning
- Felt shame when it came to money

New You:

- Knows your money personality
- Tracks your cash flow and net worth
- Has a spending plan based on your values
- Keeps cash reserves
- Uses credit intentionally
- Is building assets, not just paying bills

Even if your income hasn't changed yet.
Even if your debt isn't gone yet.
Even if nobody else sees it yet...

You are not the same.

Chapter 10: Becoming the New You

You've stepped into a new mindset.
And mindset always leads behavior.
Which means results are inevitable — *if you don't give up.*

⚡ Tips to Keep the Momentum Going

1. **Revisit Your "Why" Often**
   This isn't just about debt or savings. It's about your peace. Your future. Your freedom.
   Write your "why" somewhere visible. Let it pull you forward on hard days.

2. **Review Your Wins**
   Every debt paid. Every dollar saved. Every time you told yourself "no" to protect your "yes."
   Those are *real wins*. Stack them.

3. **Update Your Intentional Spending Plan Monthly**
   Life changes. So should your plan. Don't aim for perfect — aim for progress and alignment with your money personality.

4. **Keep a Financial Journal**
   Track what's working and what's not. Write down lessons. Process the emotions. Celebrate the growth.

5. **Stay in Community**
   Isolation is the enemy of transformation. Join, or start, a SMART Money Makeover group. Share your journey. Find accountability.

6. **Expect Setbacks — and Don't Let Them Define You**
   You'll mess up. Something unexpected will pop up. You might slip into an old pattern.
   That doesn't mean you failed. It means you're human. **Get back on track, not back in shame.**

Chapter 10: Becoming the New You

◊ A Word of Encouragement

If nobody else tells you this today, let me say it loud:

I'm proud of you.

You showed up. You faced hard truths. You didn't settle for survival. You did something most people are too scared to do — you changed.

And now, you get to build a life that aligns with your values, honors your future, and creates peace in your present.

Keep going.

👣 Final Action Step

Take a deep breath.
Then say this out loud:

"I am not who I used to be. I am the CEO of ME, Inc. I spend with intention. I grow with purpose. I build with peace. I am becoming wealthy — in every way that matters."

Now go live like it!

Coming Up Next:
The **Bonus Section** — where we'll include practical tools, conversation starters, and resources to help you share this journey with others and keep your momentum strong.

Before We Move On...

Chapter 10: Becoming the New You

If you've made it through these three sections — if you've taken the SMART system seriously, applied what you've learned about spending, saving, debt, protection, and investing — you've already set yourself up for a **stable, sustainable, and successful** financial journey.

But let me be honest with you...

I didn't learn this the easy way. I learned it the **hard** way.

Bad money moves.
Outright mistakes.
Missed opportunities.
Divorce.
And simply not knowing what I didn't know...

Those things cost me **nearly $10 million** in additional wealth that I *could* be enjoying today. Yes, I actually added it all up.

Ouch.

That's not a fun lesson. But it's one I hope you never have to experience — because you can learn from *my* mistakes. You don't have to guess your way through this.

You can **shortcut your path** to financial peace, power, and generational wealth by applying what's in these pages — and walking it out with consistency.

Now, before you go — I've got some **bonus goodies** to help you squeeze even more *pleasure* from your finances.

Let's dive into the **Bonus Section**.

Chapter 10: Becoming the New You

Chapter 10: Becoming the New You

CHAPTER 10 BONUS STORY: Pleasure At Last

ROBERT

Robert stood in line at the grocery store, holding a small cart with everything on his list — and nothing extra.

No impulse snacks. No "treat yourself" energy drinks. Just what he budgeted.

He glanced at the man ahead of him juggling three credit cards and a tired toddler. He saw his old self.

It had been a year since he picked up *SMART Money Makeover* and started over.

Chapter 10: Becoming the New You

There had been setbacks — a bounced check, a broken water pump in his car, a job change. But for once, he didn't run from it. He had a plan.

His emergency fund had $1,400.
He'd paid off two credit cards.
He knew the difference between a need and a want — and more importantly, *why* he used to blur the line.

He smiled as he tapped his debit card.

No stress.
No shame.
Just control.

Later that night, he sat at his kitchen table — cleaner now, calmer — with his notebook open.
On the top of the page, he wrote:

"SMART Money Goals – Year 2"

- Finish the debt snowball
- Save 6 months of expenses
- Take my son on a debt-free vacation

He wasn't where he wanted to be.
But he wasn't where he used to be either.
In fact, he was beginning to live the first parts of his rich life.

"I'm proud of you," he whispered to himself.
And this time… he meant it.

Chapter 10: Becoming the New You

KIA

Kia took her usual spot at the front of a small community room with a whiteboard behind her that read:

"30-Day SMART Challenge – Week 1: Self-Knowledge"

Five women sat in folding chairs, notebooks open, eyes full of uncertainty — just like hers had been.

She smiled.

"Okay, let's talk about where your money story really began…"

She walked them through money personalities, emotional triggers, and childhood beliefs. She didn't preach. She related.

Chapter 10: Becoming the New You

"I used to be a First Responder. Always giving. Never filling my own tank. But I learned to stop bleeding from a place I was supposed to be building."

After class, one woman stayed behind.
She had tears in her eyes and said,

"I didn't know people like us could learn this stuff."

Kia hugged her and said,

"That's the lie they tell us. But we know better now."

At home that night, her daughter helped her count hand-outs for the next workshop.

Her budget was no longer tight.
She had nearly doubled her income since starting the SMART Money program.
She was living her rich life at last, even taking vacations on a regular basis.
She's even considering buying her first home next year and an investment property after.

Her car still made weird noises sometimes.
But, her peace? Untouchable.
Her pain? Gone.
Her pleasure? Abounding!

Kia wasn't just surviving anymore.
She was **planting seeds** — and watching them grow in other people's lives too.

Bonus Section

Extra Tools and Tips to Bring More Pleasure to Your Financial Journey

You've done the hard part — you showed up, faced the numbers, unpacked the emotions, and laid a new foundation for your financial life.

Now let's lock it in with some **bonus resources** designed to help you **go further, faster** — and with more peace, clarity, and joy along the way.

The Money Personality Assessment

Finding Out Who You Are and Why You Do The Things You Do With Money

This assessment is something that I developed after working for over 10 years with people from all sorts of backgrounds. This second iteration was developed using additional feedback from my clients and then inputting all of that information into Ai. That produced a much more refined and intuitive assessment.

It is designed to give you a starting point for understanding how and why you relate to money the way you do. Armed with this knowledge, you can start making better, more informed money decisions that will finally get you where you want to be with your finances.

You can find the full online assessment, with guidelines for each personality, on my website's homepage at www.intentionalmoneysolutions.com

Bonus Section

💬 Money Conversation Starters
For Couples, Families & Friends

Talking about money doesn't have to be awkward or stressful — not if you approach it with curiosity and compassion. These prompts are designed to spark real, productive conversations.

For Couples:

- What did money feel like growing up in your household?
- What's one financial win you're proud of that I may not know about?
- What are three things we both value that should guide how we spend?
- What's one money-related fear you carry — and how can I support you in it?
- If we could achieve one financial goal together in the next year, what would it be?

For Families (with Kids):

- Why do you think people work and earn money?
- What's something you want to save up for?
- Why do we make choices like cooking at home instead of eating out?
- What's one way we can be generous as a family this month?

For Friends or Small Groups:

- What was your biggest money "aha" moment from this book?

Bonus Section

- Which part of the SMART system challenged you the most?
- What's one change you've made (or want to make) with your money?
- How can we keep each other accountable over the next 30 days?

Bonus Section

🛠 Recommended Tools & Resources

Your SMART Money Toolkit

Here are some practical tools to help you implement what you've learned:

Budgeting & Tracking:

- YNAB (You Need A Budget)
- EveryDollar
- Rocket Money or Monarch Money (for subscription tracking)

Saving & Investing:

- Fidelity, Vanguard, or Schwab (for long-term investing)
- Acorns or Betterment (for beginner-friendly investing)
- Ally Bank or Capital One 360 (for sinking funds or high-yield savings)

Credit Reports:

- AnnualCreditReport.com (for free reports from all three bureaus)

Credit Monitoring & Score Insights:

- Credit Karma or Credit Sesame (for ongoing score tracking)

Debt Payoff Calculators:

- Undebt.it or Dave Ramsey Snowball Calculator

Bonus Section

🤝 Dealing With Debt Collectors & Negotiating With Creditors

Because Your Peace of Mind Comes First

Here's what I tell every client:

You are not your debt. And you don't have to be bullied by it.

Tips for Handling Debt Collectors:

- **Don't panic.** Breathe. You're in control.

- **Know your rights.** Collectors must follow the Fair Debt Collection Practices Act (FDCPA). They can't harass, threaten, or call at unreasonable hours.

- **Get it in writing.** Before agreeing to anything, request a validation letter. This proves the debt is real, accurate, and still legally collectible.

- **Don't give out personal info.** Never share your bank account or debit card details over the phone.

- **Negotiate — but don't promise what you can't deliver.** Many collectors will settle for less than the full amount. Start low, and work up. Always get the agreement in writing before sending a payment.

- **Set boundaries.** You can request communication in writing only. If they're calling your job or family, that's a violation. Document everything. And NEVER pay a bill at the expense of your 5 Pillars. They will survive without your payment. You come first.

Tips for Negotiating with Creditors (Original Lenders):

- Call when you're **calm**, not desperate.

Bonus Section

- Explain your situation honestly — and have a proposed solution.
- Ask about **payment plans**, interest rate reductions, or forbearance options.
- Be polite, but firm. Document names, dates, and terms discussed.

Pro Tips for Settling with Debt Collection Agencies (The Guys Who Buy Your Debt From The Original Lender):

- Never acknowledge the debt when they call.
- Ask them to mail you "proof of debt." In other words, documentation that proves you owe this money.
- When they provide proof of debt and you have a sum of cash that you feel is doable and fair to settle the debt, then you can begin negotiating.
- First off, know that they purchased this debt for pennies on the dollar, so never offer the full amount. A good place to start would be 25% of the original debt.
- Play hardball. Let them know that you have this amount, cash in hand, to send them to settle the debt in full. Tell them that you are seeking settlement with all your creditors and if they do not want to accept your offer, you will take your money and offer it to someone who is willing to make a deal with you.
- Stand firm, hold your ground and maintain your peace of mind.

Bottom line? **You get to protect your peace.** You're allowed to set limits, ask questions, and take control of the conversation.

Bonus Section

📊 Credit Score Boosting Tips

Small Habits = Big Impact

1. **Pay everything on time.** Payment history makes up 35% of your score.

2. **Keep credit utilization below 30%.** Even better? Under 10%.

3. **Don't close old accounts.** Age of credit matters — keep those seasoned lines open.

4. **Dispute errors.** Check your reports and challenge anything that's inaccurate.

5. **Become an authorized user.** If someone trustworthy has great credit, being added to their card (with no expectation to use it) can boost your score.

6. **Use a secured credit card if rebuilding.** Start small and pay it off every month.

Remember, boosting your score doesn't happen overnight — but **steady steps** create real progress over time.

🔖 **BONUS** Resource: You can get your Credit Repair Checklist PDF at https://intentionalmoneysolutions.com/resources/

Bonus Section

📓 Book Club / Small Group Guide

Share the Journey, Multiply the Growth

Want to go deeper with friends, your partner, or your community? Start a **SMART Money Makeover** group!

Here's a suggested **6-week format**:

Week 1: Introduction + Your Money Story
Week 2: Money Personalities + Self-Knowledge
Week 3: Cash Flow + Net Worth + Awareness
Week 4: Allocated Spending & Intentional Spending Plans
Week 5: Emergency Funds + Debt Freedom
Week 6: Credit, Insurance, Investing & Next Steps

Make space for vulnerability, practical takeaways, and fun. Celebrate progress — not perfection.

Bonus Section

🎯 Coaching & Next Steps

Want Help Making Your SMART Money Makeover Stick?

If you want to take your financial transformation to the next level, I offer:

- **1-on-1 Coaching** – Personalized guidance to walk you through your journey
- **Workshops & Group Coaching** – Learn in a community and gain accountability
- **Business & Entrepreneurial Strategy** – For those building a legacy beyond their paycheck

📩 Visit www.IntentionalMoneySolutions.com or follow us on the following platforms:

YouTube: @IntentionalMoneySolutions

Facebook: @IntentionalMoneySolutions

Instagram: @forrest_huguenin/

Threads: @forrest_huguenin

TikTok: @forresthuguenin

LinkeIn: @forrest-huguenin-648480b/

Bonus Section

Final Words From Forrest

I truly hope you found hope and a plan inside these pages. I know that when I was at the end of my rope, that's exactly what I needed. I read some books and it helped me gain hope and get a plan together. But it was a long, hard road of trial and error and struggle before I finally got my act together.

And did you see yourself in either Robert or Kia?

To all the Roberts out there: I see you and I feel you. It can be hard to admit when we're wrong and it can be even harder to actually change. I was you. But I changed. And if you follow the advice in this book, you can't help but change. So, just get started with the first step and see the benefits. Once you see one win, you won't be able to stop rolling along!

To all the Kias out there: If you're a single parent trying to keep the lights on and food on the table, you are awesome. Your kids need you to keep showing up every day and showing them love and setting an example they will never forget. Keep at that side hustle until it becomes a full-blown successful business that eventually replaces your full-time income. Keep earning, keep learning, keep growing. You got this!

Finally, if no one has told you lately:

I'm proud of you.

You showed up for yourself. You stared down old habits. You chose to believe there's a better way — and now, you've got the tools to walk it out.

I wrote this book so you wouldn't have to lose years and millions like I did. So you could learn what I wish I had learned *sooner*.

And I wrote it so you can leave financial pain behind in the trash bin where it belongs and step confidently into financial pleasure.

Final Words From Forrest

**Keep going. You are the CEO of YOU, Inc.
And this company? It's headed toward incredible, generational wealth!**

About The Author

Forrest Huguenin grew up in Queens, NY in a lower middle-class household. His early career was spent learning computers and facilities management in various institutional banks.

From there, he spent an extensive amount of time in sales, financial advisory and real estate.

Along the way he, like many, experienced ups and downs in a constant struggle to develop a healthy relationship with money.

He is intimately familiar with what financial pain means and what it takes to battle back and come through the other side to financial pleasure.

Over a period that spanned more than 2 decades, he has personally coached others, written books, created courses and given countless webinars and seminars on the subject of personal finance.

From all that experience came this book, SMART Money Makeover.

He currently resides on Long Island.

His mission in life remains to help spare others the pain he experienced trying to get the mastery over his own finances.

If you have similar struggles with money or just feel like you should have more to show financially for all your hard work, schedule a free discovery session with him at www.intentionalmoneysolutions.com.

www.ingramcontent.com/pod-product-compliance
Lightning Source LLC
Chambersburg PA
CBHW072049290426
44110CB00014B/1603